POLICE FIREARMS INSTRUCTION

PROBLEMS AND PRACTICES

POLICE FIREARMS INSTRUCTION

PROBLEMS AND PRACTICES

RICHARD GRASSI

Foreword by Massad Ayoob

CRC Press
Taylor & Francis Group
Boca Raton London New York

CRC Press is an imprint of the
Taylor & Francis Group, an **informa** business

CRC Press
Taylor & Francis Group
6000 Broken Sound Parkway NW, Suite 300
Boca Raton, FL 33487-2742

Printed in the United States of America on acid-free paper
10 9 8 7 6 5 4 3 2 1

International Standard Book Number-13: 978-1-4200-6506-0 (Hardcover)

Library of Congress Cataloging-in-Publication Data

Grassi, Richard.
Police firearms instruction : problems and practices / Richard Grassi.
p. cm.
Includes bibliographical references and index.
ISBN 978-1-4200-6506-0 (hardback : alk. paper) 1. Police training--United States--Handbooks, manuals, etc. 2. Firearms--Use in crime prevention--Study and teaching--United States--Handbooks, manuals, etc. 3. Grassi, Richard. 4. Police--United States--Biography. I. Title.

HV8142.G73 2008
363.2'3--dc22 2008015640

Visit the Taylor & Francis Web site at
http://www.taylorandfrancis.com

and the CRC Press Web site at
http://www.crcpress.com

Dedication

To those who have gone before us, to those who've helped me along and to all the dedicated instructors who work tirelessly to get their people home at the day's end.

In Memoriam

Thomas Daniel Rhyne, sergeant, Shawnee County Sheriff's Department, September 20, 1998: Instructor, mentor, friend

Norman Grassi, July 31, 2003: My very first firearms instructor, my father and friend

Nancy Grassi Wickes, June 18, 2004

Harland M. Bonner, deputy sheriff, Morehouse Parish (Louisiana) Sheriff's Department, Bastrop, Louisiana: June 22, 1984

John Dean Cooper, founder, API: September 25, 2006

James Cirillo, New York City Police Department, retired, mentor and friend: July 12, 2007

Foreword

Rich Grassi has emerged as one of our most logical and influential instructors in police weapons and officer survival training. I've watched him develop over the years and am in a position to say that he has done a lot of good. I was happy when I was able to shanghai him into joining the Firearms Committee of the American Society of Law Enforcement Trainers (ASLET). He was an asset there and has proven to be such to every department, every training organization, and every publisher who has been fortunate enough to tap into his hard-earned experience and wisdom.

There are a lot of books out there that purport to make you a teacher of these things. Once you get into them, you find that most will have much to say about how to perform a given discipline but little to say on how to impart it to others. The volume in your hands right now is a genuine "how to teach it" book, and that makes it priceless.

Note that Rich tells you something about his background early on. That's not to give you his autobiography; it's to show that what trainers bring to the table when they receive a teaching assignment is going to help shape the prism through which they view their duties and responsibilities.

You don't have to be a champion shooter to be a fine instructor in combat shooting. I've seen some world champs—Frank Garcia, Rob Leatham, and Ray Chapman, among others—who were also master instructors and loved to share what they had learned. But I've also seen some who just couldn't transmit their knowledge, some who had no patience for those on a lower skill level than their own, and a very few who didn't even *want* to share their knowledge because they thought of it as their personal secret weapon. On the other end of the spectrum, I never quite bought the old saying, "The instructor can be a lousy shot so long as he's a good teacher." If he can't teach *himself*, how the hell is he going to successfully teach a separate human organism? For what it's worth, though I've never seen Rich Grassi at a match, I've seen him many times on the range and can assure you that he's a helluva good shot.

I can remember when a few others and I felt like voices in the wilderness when we called for integrated use of force training back in the '70s. Today, it has become the new paradigm, and Rich Grassi and men and women like him had a huge part in making that happen. I remember the day in Kansas City when I introduced Rich to Jim Lindell…and how proud I was later when Jim told me Rich had become one of his most valued trainers of other instructors in the life-saving discipline Jim had created.

We all whimper, "We need more time and budget for training, and the chief won't give it to us." In this book, Rich shows you how to present arguments and budgets that will satisfy even the most tightly sphinctered bean-counters, and get those extra rounds and hours approved by high command. He doesn't waste time cursing the darkness; Grassi lights a torch and shows you how to light your own.

There's no bombast in Rich Grassi. He's a soft-spoken man with a dry sense of humor. He is also an inspirational teacher, even if he manages to accomplish that without raising his voice.

He has to inspire. It's his duty. And if you teach these things, it's your duty too; it's a thread that runs throughout this book. You need a fire in your belly to teach these disciplines. The bored instructor—the one who does "just enough"—won't do society that much damage if he's teaching something less important. We, however, are *the teachers of staying alive!* If we fail to light a fire in the belly of each and every student—a fire fueled with reality, with alertness and awareness, with the will to fight and prevail—then somewhere down the road, some young man or woman who counted on us will die because we didn't give him or her the inspiration needed to maintain constant capability and vigilance in a very dangerous job.

I believe this book is destined to be a classic on the desks of police trainers in weapons and use of force. Particularly if you are new to your instructorship, pore over it and give it your closest attention. Rich has done what you're now doing. There is much you can learn from him.

Enjoy the book. Absorb the book. Use it to help those who trust you to stay alive and unhurt. Channel the good advice Rich Grassi gives you, and learn among other things why those of us privileged to know and work with Rich are proud to call him a friend and colleague.

Keep your people safe. Godspeed.

Massad Ayoob

Massad Ayoob has been a police firearms instructor since the early 1970s, and later became an international instructor in the PR-24 baton and a national instructor for Jim Lindell at the National Law Enforcement Training Center in Kansas City. Mas is the founder (1981) and director of Lethal Force Institute, and the author of several books and training films, and thousands of articles on armed and unarmed self-defense, law enforcement, and related topics. He served more than 19 years as chair of the Firearms Committee of ASLET.

Preface

This book is intended to be a "seminar" in law enforcement firearms instruction. Few of the items discussed are cast in stone as far as I'm concerned. There's lots of fluidity and room for investigation and change.

The reason for the book is straightforward: There are lots of agency firearms instructors across the United States who have had very little formal training in firearms, in shooting, and in teaching. To supplement this, most instructors have access only to gun magazines. A few state associations of firearms instructors exist and trainers located in those states are lucky.

In some states, you can be designated as the firearms instructor by your agency's chief executive to be the rangemaster, with no formal training whatsoever required in those states.

Few officers with firearms instructor duties get to go to training seminars and conferences. For those of us who do or did, we ended up paying most of the way ourselves. There was no money budgeted for continuing education.

I learned much at conferences and seminars put on by ASLET (American Society of Law Enforcement Trainers, now defunct) and IALEFI (International Association of Law Enforcement Firearms Instructors). At those meetings, I'd come away realizing that the problems we faced at home were the same ones that all of us faced across the country and around the world.

I'd pick up a drill, exercise, lecture topic, or range setup idea that I'd pilfer and take home. This book is peppered with such items. It's a buffet; go along the line. Take what pleases you. Change it to fit the needs of your agency and your situation. Disagree with some of it? Let's talk. Let's advance the common knowledge, skills, and abilities and make us all better at this most important of jobs.

The only thing between a cop and the grave is skill—skill at reading people, at observation, at caution and sneakiness, and skill at arms. The way most of our people get skill is by seeing the example of their trainers and instructors. We owe it to them to be the best we can be.

So let's start our seminar!

Acknowledgments

This book is written as a reflection of what I learned from many people over many years. A number of them are mentioned inside the chapters of this book—in fact, they gave me the basis of what appears herein.

Some of them I haven't seen in years—including Clive Shepherd, the wily Royal Marine and world-class instructor; Vince O'Neill (Oklahoma Council on Law Enforcement Education and Training [CLEET]); and Gene Zink and John Meyer (late of the Heckler & Koch International Training Division). Others I get to see on rare occasion, such as Mike Dunlap (Amarillo Police Department, Texas), Mike Boyle (New Jersey Game and Fish, retired), Boyce Moses (Kansas Law Enforcement Training Center), Walter Rauch (former U.S. Secret Service), Hans Vang (Vangcomp Systems), and John Delgado (Miami-Dade County Police Department, retired).

The basis for the shooting skills component of the book came from the groundbreakers—Jim Cirillo and Jeff Cooper, both recently lost to us, and Massad Ayoob. Conduits for their knowledge include Giles and Ed Stock, Larry Mudgett, Dave Harris, Chris Weare, Bob Smith, and Marty and Gila Hayes.

The tactical training began for me with Dick Lee and Dan Rhyne, both of the Shawnee County Sheriff's Department. They took me under their collective wing and brought me along. Mas Ayoob continued the mentoring process, which led to Clive Shepherd during his National Rifle Association (NRA) tour of duty. Mas was also responsible for getting me together with James Lindell, friend, mentor, teacher, and developer of the Handgun/Long Gun Retention and Disarming System, as well as founder of the National Law Enforcement Training Center, Kansas City, Missouri.

Bruce Cameron, then-editor of *Law and Order*, taught me to write to a law enforcement audience. Harry Kane, editor in the Harris Outdoors Group, helped me polish the prose and taught me how to take a photograph. Contributions to my relative skill level were made by Mike Rafferty, Harry Carpenter, Jerry Lee, Marshal Schmitt, Dennis Tueller, Dave Spaulding, John Visintini, and Bob Radecki.

The friendship of Mark and Stephanie Fricke (American Firearms Training and Tactics [AFTT], Prescott Valley, Arizona), Denny Hansen (editor, *SWAT* magazine), Ralph and Joan Holtzhaus (The Wilderness Tactical), Lou Alessi, Buzz Mills, Tom Marx, Bill Wilson, Chuck Buis, Richard Davis (Armor Express), Gregg Garrett (Comp-Tac), Mark Garrity (Garrity's

Gunleather), Scott Carnahan, Paul Pluff and Joe Bergeron (both of Smith & Wesson), and from many friends in the shooting and outdoors industry was of huge importance.

The driving force behind my modest success is provided selflessly by my wife, Jane Grassi—the best partner I could ever have. Without her, this project wouldn't exist.

The Author

Richard Grassi went into law enforcement after a term of service with the U.S. Army. While working as a peace officer, first in Pittsburg, Kansas, and then as a deputy in the Shawnee County Sheriff's Department (Topeka), he attained his bachelor's and master's degrees. He taught classes at the Washburn University Criminal Justice Department and became the first full-time training coordinator at the Shawnee County Sheriff's Office. While serving as a sheriff's deputy, he supervised detectives and narcotics officers, wrote the general order dealing with use of force, and organized and taught the agency's transition to a new weapon system.

Grassi is a writer and trainer in the areas of firearms, police use of force, and defensive tactics. Honorably retired from law enforcement, he remains a named instructor at the annual National Law Enforcement Training Center Seminar, where he certifies Lindell handgun retention instructors. He is published regularly in national publications, including *Combat Handguns*, *Guns & Weapons for Law Enforcement*, and *Special Weapons for Military and Police*. His writing career began with *Police Marksman* and *Law and Order*.

His professional affiliations include International Association of Law Enforcement Firearms Instructors (IALEFI), American Society of Law Enforcement Trainers (ASLET), National Rifle Association (life member), National Law Enforcement Training Center (national trainer—instructor trainer), Kansas Peace Officers Association (KPOA) member, Fraternal Order of Police, Lodge #3, Topeka.

Grassi's professional certifications include: Kansas Law Enforcement Training Center firearms instructor, National Rifle Association Law Enforcement firearms instructor, tactical shooting instructor, Kansas concealed carry handgun instructor, Kansas Attorney General's Office, deadly force instructor, Lethal Force Institute, Glock armorer, Ruger P-series pistol and subgun armorer, advanced firearms instructor/Heckler & Koch (HK): Gunsite.

Contents

Burning Powder: Philosophy and Values

1

Any discussion of firearms use has to include a warning and an injunction. Here's mine:

Firearms use can be dangerous, particularly by those who are untrained or lightly trained. This book *does not* take the place of hands-on training! If you try to do some of the things listed in this book strictly from reading this book and without the assistance of a trainer, coach, or instructor, you can be injured or killed!

As a matter of record, I learned under the watchful eye of a mentor, trainer, and coach. Norman Grassi, my father, took me under his wing and tried to instill in me some values. His success came over time, not all at once.

A veteran of a childhood in the Great Depression and military experience in World War II (European theater), he carried in him an enduring respect for life. I recall a few things from our time together relevant to this discussion.

Figure 1.1 Having the ability to keep students' attention, even during lectures, is the mark of the pro. Clive Shepherd is shown here during an international conference.

Safety

My first encounter with firearms involved Dad and me "goin' shootin'," as he put it. The object was an old Stevens long-barrel rimfire rifle chambered for .22 short-long-long rifle. It was occasionally capable of semiautomatic operation with long-rifle (LR) ammo. We used .22 shorts for basic training. While it wasn't silent, the report was scarcely noticeable in the strip-mined land (strip pits) we used as a range.

The first lesson was loading and unloading, followed by the concept of not shooting over the horizon. He explained that the bullet could travel about a mile and still have the power to penetrate a human body, potentially killing someone I couldn't see.

He said never to point a gun at anyone and told me how dangerous the "unloaded" gun could be—accidents always seemed to happen with "unloaded" guns. The gun's safety was not to be relied on. Such mechanisms had failed before.

Dad said to make sure I knew what I was shooting at and to make sure no one was near the mark or behind it. A bullet could perforate the target and go on to hit someone behind it.

Philosophy

He was far-sighted, able to see and identify birds at some distance. On one occasion, a shooting foray turned into a revealing discussion about his take on life. He'd hunted for much of his life but found himself incapable of taking deer. He preferred birds to rabbits and squirrels. But even then, he confessed, he felt a small part of himself die when he shot a mourning dove.

A young fool, I didn't understand what he was telling me until he taught me to hunt. The first dove I took created a strangely mixed feeling of elation and sadness. A bond between us was created that has yet to end, in spite of his passing. A common experience demonstrated his humanity, his compassion, and his ability to reach out by teaching.

As I originally wrote this section, he was nearing 80 years of age. The lessons he taught formed the foundation for the rest of my life. Whatever I am, whatever I become, arises from our shared experience—the spoken word and the demonstration. My drive to become a firearms instructor comes in large measure from this basis.

Ethics, honesty, and fair play are all components of his approach. They are components of my approach as well.

Guns and Teaching

I continued my firearms experience in a public school—something hardly likely in this enlightened time. A student in Army Junior ROTC, we were exposed to the M1 and M14 rifles. We used a number of Winchester target .22 rifles in a 50-foot indoor range under Parkwood High School. I lacked a lot of skill at the position competition, scoring NRA Smallbore Expert only once.

My mother wasn't a fan of firearms but did nothing to dissuade me from them, supporting my habit and my ROTC affiliation.

As I passed through my high school years and through staff positions, I eventually became an assistant instructor. I'd been battalion adjutant and had little time left in school. With a group of other seniors, I began to learn the Army way of teaching. I took my first class in methods of instruction.

It was an invaluable experience in learning how to teach. The focus is on the learner, while the responsibility for success rests with the instructor. A few examples of the "lecture" format follow:

1. Empty your pockets. If you are handling change while you speak to the group, someone will wonder how much change you have and won't focus on the lesson.
2. Take off your watch and place it on the lectern. Glance at your watch while "reloading" your memory from lecture notes while speaking. In this way, you can judge time without having the class wonder what time it is.
3. Don't use the lectern for cover. Move, but never turn your back on the audience. Walk in "Vs" and "Ws." Make frequent eye contact.
4. If you use chalk—remember, this was in the days before whiteboards—to write or to make a graphic, put it down when you've finished writing. To keep it in your hand and gesture with it interferes with the message.
5. Keep a cover over the slide on the overhead projector. (There was no PowerPoint in those days either.) Reveal only the line you're referring to as you go along.
6. Do not read from the visual aid or handouts. The students can read. If there's one who can't read, he or she belongs in a reading class.

The problem with this was that, as high school students, we began to critique our teachers! As a result of the training, I watched other speakers, instructors, and even television evangelists to see for myself what worked and, more important, what didn't.

When taking a university basic philosophy course about 5 years later, I noticed something about the professor. He entered the room and deposited

Figure 1.2 The ability to demonstrate the skills students are required to emulate is critical to success.

his notes on the lectern. He removed his watch and placed it by his notes. He then emptied his pockets on a table near the lectern.

Following the "tell them what you're going to teach, teach it, tell them what you taught" method, he'd use chalk and stow it as soon as he stopped writing. Using his teaching protocol, my notes were organized and I was able to pass the course handily—though I didn't "ace" it.

Military Years

After high school, I entered the U.S. Army. I wasn't really a very good soldier, but I got away with an honorable discharge. My tour was undistinguished, all of it stateside. I was awarded the Army Commendation Medal (ARCOM) for showing up to work and not being too much a fool. I was never in Special Forces, Rangers, or Airborne, which can be detrimental to a firearms instructor's reputation because there are so many in the training field who have had such experiences.

I didn't get the opportunity to try out for the Marksmanship Training Unit (MTU) and, in retrospect, I don't know that I could have made the cut. I visited the Army MTU in Fort Benning while assigned there. I was given the grand tour and found members of the unit to be friendly and forthcoming. It was my first exposure to Running Boar, a moving target competition.

I also got to shoot an original M1873 Springfield .45-70—with black powder loads, naturally.

I moved on to another post and met the operations sergeant in our S3 shop. He'd been an MTU member and was quite a shot. He knew "the Deal"* and was happy to share. He briefed me on his time in Vietnam, telling innocuous war stories. He spoke of no bloody battles but of plinking with a Thompson submachine gun (SMG) on a firebase.

He helped me set up a 1911 of dubious history. At his suggestion, I attended the matches on post and picked the brains of the shooters. I quickly became a brass rat, picking the empties up to the shooters' delight. Buckets of .38 Special brass (from midrange wadcutters) and .45 ACP (Automatic Colt Pistol) brass went home with me.

It was a short step to reloading and to hobby shooting. I came into a 6-inch Colt Python early on—I still have it. A pair of .357 Ruger Blackhawks made it into the stable.

These Rugers were 3-screw Blackhawks. Some years before the New Model appeared, these had to be carried hammer-down on an empty chamber.

A few years of shooting and reloading ended during an undergraduate tour of duty at my hometown university. To make ends meet, I signed on with my hometown police department.

Entry-Level Police

My first range experience was an eye-opener. As I relate in Chapter 2, I'd learned much of my pistol technique from books and magazines—not the wisest way to go about such things.

I'd come into possession of a Colt National Match .45 from a city resident who'd been a town cop. He needed the money, I needed the gun. The magazines, as it turned out, were "gun show specials."

Officers at the department had to provide their own guns at that time, and there was something of a "big boy" rule: you could carry it if you could qualify with it.

At this first range experience, I was put on the line with no briefing and no preparation. This was in the days before agencies put the new hires through training before putting them on the street. I tried to shoot the course and the Colt NM "jammed."

Honestly, I knew no better. A gent named Harry Claflin was present. At that time, he was proprietor of the Starlight Training Center over in Missouri.

* In physical skills, the Deal is simply knowing enough to do it. A shooter who can hit the mark knows the Deal. A defensive tactics student who can correctly demonstrate blocks and strikes likewise knows the Deal.

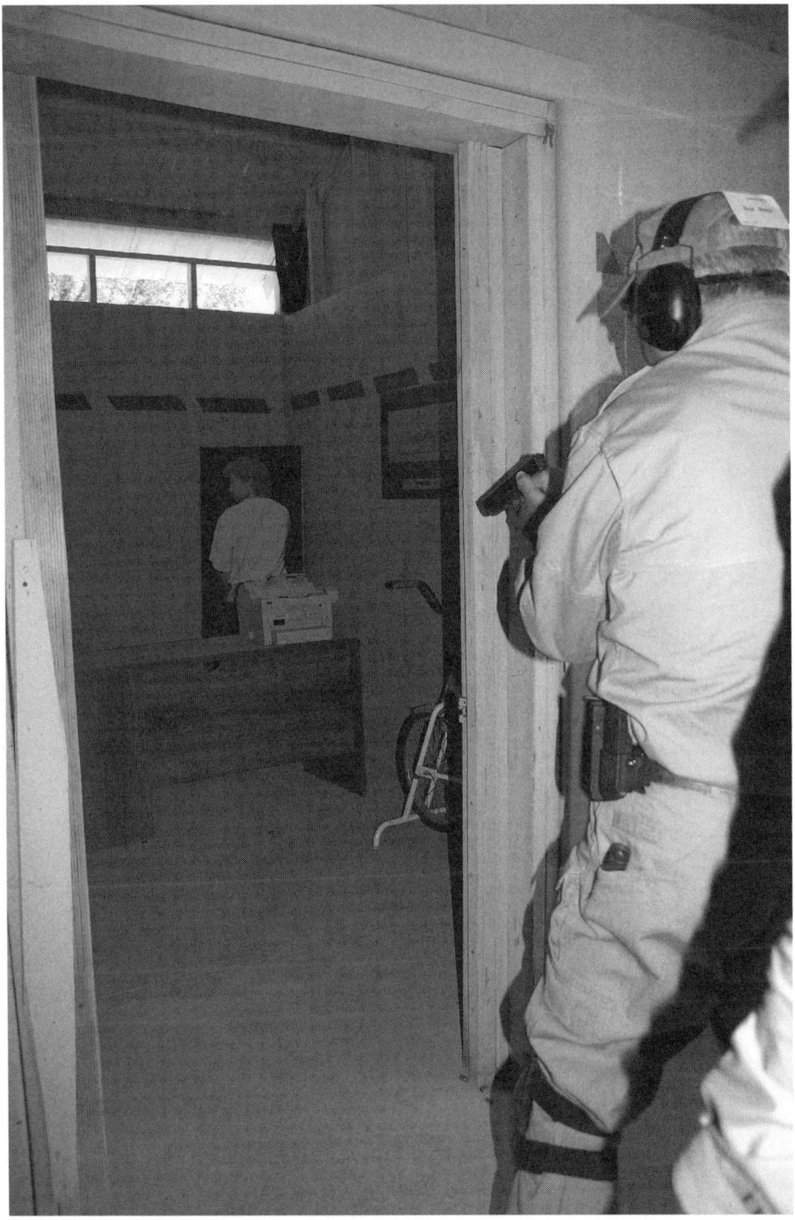

Figure 1.3 Our people face challenges of all kinds on the street. They have to face those challenges in training *first*. Rehearsal is important.

He did a "factory adjustment" to one of the magazines and tossed another out. He fronted me enough ammo to finish the course and gave me some advice. My memory's dim, but I think I got a 96% score—with his guidance and assistance.

Figure 1.4 Master firearms instructors (from left to right) Jim Cirillo, NYPD retired; Dan Rhyne, Topeka Sheriff's Department; and nationally known trainer and author Massad Ayoob, all sharpening their skills at a training conference.

My style was okay, but it seemed to take forever to reload the pistol. Harry showed me his technique, which he'd, no doubt, picked up elsewhere.

My early police career was fun and it enabled me to get an undergraduate degree. I got onto our pistol team one season and took the Novice Award at the Kansas Peace Officers Association in spring 1978. I'd also begun to compete in steel target matches in northeast Oklahoma gravel pits. It was there that I met Bill Wilson, now the president of Wilson Combat.

A friendly sort, Wilson was as fast as lightning and more than accurate enough to beat all contestants, including me. It was great fun and my first real exposure to speed shooting.

I ended up in Topeka employed by the airport police. I'd been selected to go to the state's firearms instructor school. I'd picked up an annoying flinch along the way, so I was ably coached by an affable lieutenant, Harland "Bo" Bonner. He spent quite a bit of time working with me to try to correct that affliction.

He subsequently left to go home to Bastrop, Louisiana. A deputy sheriff there, Bo arrested a subject on a misdemeanor warrant. The offender was able to snatch Bo's gun and murder him.

Stunned by this event, I vowed to work to prevent this kind of thing from happening again. It was the least I could do for the coach who'd helped me out so much.

Figure 1.5 See the logo on his shirt? Your people need to read that. Train like your life depends on it—because it does!

Badges and Bullets

2

I don't know that I'd have gotten involved in police work if it weren't for the nexus with firearms. I was already an enthusiast. But combined with a deep curiosity about everything that went on—the real prerequisite to a police career—the guns got me in.

Pre-Police Gunfire

I had some shooting experience before my police service. Dad had shown me that the "ball" (front sight) had to be placed into the "U" notch rear blade on his old Stevens, and that image had to be superimposed onto the mark. The system was tin-can accurate as long as I didn't slap at the trigger. My sole handgun experience had been with an uncle's Harrington & Richardson (H&R) double-action .22 revolver. I recall how stiff the trigger was and how much louder it was than the old, long-barrel Stevens rifle.

Another adult lent me a nickel-plated Colt .22 single action Frontier Scout. The rear notch in the frame was square and the front sight appeared square when looking at it through the notch. The trigger was much better than the H&R, though the plating made the sights shiny.

I put a few bricks of .22 LR through that revolver and learned something. While I was about it, I learned that such guns needed to be carried with "five beans in the wheel." The hammer was lowered on an empty chamber. There was no transfer bar or hammer block, so a dropped gun could fire.

Even today, when I evaluate single-action revolvers for articles, I load them the old-fashioned way. There's no way to tell if I'll come into possession of an old-model gun that needs such treatment.

While in high school, I fired .22 Winchester target rifles in the basement range of the school. Having a shooting range in a school might sound shocking to some, but I approve of the concept.

These target rifles had peep sights fore and aft. The smaller diameter tube forward was centered in the rear aperture and the bull was centered in the front tube. Later, in military service, I had to learn about the peep and post sights on the XM16E2—the rifles we had in basic training.

My primary interest was handguns. They were, by all accounts, harder to learn to use well. Our hometown public library was well stocked for reading on this topic. I routinely checked out Chic Gaylord's 1960 book,

Figure 2.1 Old school: This officer began work in the middle of the 20th century. His long-barrel Python is holstered in an extreme drop holster specially made for this user. He was a motorcycle officer.

Handgunner's Guide. (To see current renditions of his holster designs, go to http://bellcharteroakholsters.com/index.htm.)

Another author I read during the period was John Dean "Jeff" Cooper. He wrote *Complete Book of Modern Handgunning* and *Fighting Handguns*, both of which we had in the local library, and I found that he was still being published in magazines. Over the years, Mr. Cooper's technique began to look less and less like Mr. Gaylord's. I studied his work closely, in part due to the difference between the two styles of shooting.

Instead of shooting one-handed from a crouch, pictures of Cooper showed him standing erect, using two hands on the gun. In my own experiments with handguns, I found that I had superior hits with Cooper's technique.

Many years later, I attended a class at Cooper's ranch. He'd started his American Pistol Institute on a place he called Gunsite. Still in operation today, Gunsite is the home of his doctrine, known as the modern technique of the pistol. As I'd learned from his writing and later reinforced at Gunsite, his technique included:

1. The Weaver stance and grip,
2. The flash sight picture, and
3. The compressed surprise break.

Critics seem to focus on the stance and the use of the front sight. I did the same thing. The hardest element to learn, articulate, and teach is the compressed surprise break. As I was to find out, trigger control is the Holy Grail.

Modern Technique

Cooper's view was that appropriate, free-style competition was the means to determine the best personal defense tools and techniques. To do that, the match has to simulate combat.

You don't want to take a small caliber handgun into a fight. If bigger is better, you compete with the bigger caliber. Would you carry light target ammunition on duty? If you carry full-power service ammunition, compete with it.

If you have a fast-draw holster on the range but you carry concealed, how does the range work help you with your ultimate objective?

In his analysis, started during his Big Bear Lake days, whatever was the most quickly accurate won the match. This was in the time of television westerns and detective shows where everyone shot from the hip. During fast-draw competitions, you could "make the quickest noise" from the hip. When it came to hitting a target—say, a balloon—you could still make a quick noise—the gunshot.

Figure 2.2 The classic Weaver stance is shown here: The gun arm is straight or slightly bent with the non-gun arm bent with the elbow at 6 o'clock. There is isometric tension between the hands—the gun hand pushes toward the muzzle while the non-gun hand pulls back. Thumbs are high in the Weaver grip. This 4-inch Colt Python in .357 Magnum is easily controlled by Weaver.

The shooter who hit the most and the quickest was deputy sheriff Jack Weaver. He had a relaxed stance, used two hands on the gun—an S&W K-38—held at eye level. His arms were bent.

As Cooper tried this out, he found that he was quicker to recover from recoil when he used isometric tension in the Weaver stance. The gun hand pushes forward while the non-gun hand pulls the gun hand toward the shooter. Do it in the extreme and the hands shake—isometric tension. Settle off just a little and you have a quick shooting, quick recovering stance.

Sights

Similarly, Cooper used a visual focus on the front sight to confirm the direction of the muzzle and its relationship to the target. It was a simple matter to look at the target until the gun obstructed your view and then shift your focus from the target (threat) to the front sight.

The idea behind the flash sight picture is simple. Some have tried to make it more "simple" by the concept of "flash front sight." It seems to involve the chanting of the phrase "flash front sight" while somehow believing the student will just do it.

Figure 2.3 The Weaver was historically displayed as an upright stance. This instructor (Giles Stock) is demonstrating the position here.

Consider the target shooter. Taking a sidearm in hand, he angles his body away from the target (presenting a side view to it) and uses that stiff arm to present the pistol up through the target—through, above, and settling down onto it. The vision is on the front sight, allowing the bull's-eye to blur. A steady hold and open-ended surprise break of the trigger is all that is needed to steer a bullet into the target.

Peace officers don't require that level of precision, holding onto a mark smaller than a saucer at a distance of 75 feet. Officers are required to put hits into a circle about the size of a paper plate at about 10% of that distance. They have to do it starting from the gun in the holster and arms held naturally. Often, having to shoot is a surprise.

Figure 2.4 From the front, the Weaver looks like this: The fingers of the non-gun hand wrap around the front of the grip frame atop the fingers of the shooting hand. The non-gun elbow is bent and down.

Instead of 10 hits in 10 minutes—the slow-fire stage in bull's-eye practice—they have a second or two to realize there is a deadly threat, where it is, to present the defensive weapon to the threat, and to trigger fight-stopping hits into that threat.

A loving appreciation of the finely cut serrations in the front sight isn't necessary. It's not even wanted. All we want is a visual confirmation of what we *feel*—the muzzle is directed into the center of the threat. Like training wheels, the sights are there to support and confirm our presentation and our hold. After hours of practice and preparation, it becomes a reflexive response.

Allow the Gun to Fire

The modern idea of trigger control starts from a target shooter's perspective. The target shooter puts constantly increasing pressure on the trigger, mashing it straight back into the rear of the trigger guard, until the hammer falls. The trick is to do this without disturbing alignment of muzzle to target. The key is surprise. You know the gun will fire. You're intending that it fire. You just don't know exactly *when* it will fire.

Making this appropriate to battle means compressing the time it takes to do a surprise break. The time isn't open ended. The offender is the one who drives the need for speed.

Compressing the surprise break means just what is says—making that target-precise shot happen quickly, keeping your surprise intact. The shot will break at some point between now and then; visualize a few feet of distance between now and then. To compress the process, the distance between now and then is in fractions of an inch. The exact instant of ignition is not known to the shooter.

If the shooter knows when the shot will break, he or she will almost invariably look over the gun at the target or will compensate for recoil before it happens—causing the shot to go low and to the shooter's left, if he or she is right-handed.

Don't *make* it fire. As my mentor, Royal Marine Colour Sergeant Clive Shepherd, was known to say, "*Let* it fire."

The Combat Triad

Cooper saw survival in battle as being the result of the user's competence in elements of the Combat Triad. The Combat Triad is possessed of mind-set, marksmanship, and gun handling.

Mind-set is explained in Chapter 13. Marksmanship and gun handling are strewn throughout this work. Marksmanship is usually known as the ability to hit a mark. In battle, marksmanship is the ability to make quick, repetitive hits while facing your own mortality. It's not a matter of splitting a playing card edgeways. Instead, it's putting quick hits into the center of a human threat before that threat can take your life.

Gun handling is now commonly called "running the gun." This is a matter of being able to positively, confidently, safely, and quickly employ the weapon as well as keep that weapon in firing condition—while people are shooting at you. The elements are of equal importance. If you are in a state of constant readiness and have superb marksmanship skills under pressure, an inability to quickly eliminate a stoppage can lead to your demise.

Stoppages don't happen on every occasion you try to use a gun. They seem to happen when you're least capable of diagnosing and fixing it. Similarly, if you can hit a shot glass on demand at 10 yards while being pelted with paintballs and can reliably do two-second reloads, you're in great shape. That is, unless you are caught unaware. If you walk into an armed robbery in progress, oblivious to the fact, those skills matter far less.

Similarly, the aware gun-handling guru who can stack hits atop one another all day but can't do so under stress is also in serious trouble. It's not "two out of three isn't bad;" it's "all or nothing."

Stress Complications

Like any trained skill, the modern technique may not work for everyone. In fact, not all people we get on the job will be good at the marksmanship and gun-handling aspects. They may be good enough, but they won't have the competence of cops who have a genuine interest in and devotion to firearms excellence. Attempting to teach a skill that some believe is contrary to stress-induced responses in the undertrained can lead to frustration.

Figure 2.5 In these "enlightened" times, the Weaver is demonstrated with knees bent and shoulders ahead of the waist—"nose over the toes."

Most of our people are undertrained in skills at arms. Many of the command rank didn't like firearms training when they started the job. It's unlikely they acquired a taste for it as they worked up the organizational ladder. In addition, we have

Figure 2.6 A close-up of the classic Weaver grip shows the power of the hold on the gun. In this variation, the thumbs are still high but presented forward toward the muzzle.

students who are forced to be in training (what little training there is) and they complain upstairs. We might not be able to give them more comfortable uniforms or increase pay or benefits, but we can cut the firearms training and remove one point of contention.

This is a thorny issue, but one potential solution is to use a firearms training system that uses a range of techniques—the better to find the technique that fits each of our problem shooters.

Using the stress-response model, firearms trainer, author, and competitor Massad Ayoob developed StressFire. He sought techniques that fed off the stress response and actually worked better when you were being attacked. That it enjoyed some success is apparent by adoption of the course by the U.S. Army and a number of other agencies.

3 Stress-Reinforced Technique

Human Stress Response

After training as a deadly force instructor, instructed by Massad Ayoob, as well as taking defensive tactics instructor and homicide investigation training, I have come to some understanding of what happens to the human animal when faced with sudden extermination.

There isn't a lot of reflection. Although some people relate that there is a replay of one's life, many others describe conditions that most of us have had some small experience with.

A joke goes around about having moist palms and a dry mouth—as opposed to the normal condition of dry palms and a less dry mouth. Nausea and the sweats can accompany the near-death experience, as well as the "shakes." Very often people who survive—often in no part due to their own efforts—express disbelief or surprise. Cooper described it as a strong urge to "change the channel."

"This *can't* be happening" is one expression of the feeling. Or, my own, "Oh, damn! I should have known."

Operating System

The body's alarm reaction comes on when the mind has determined that deadly danger is imminent. An instructor of mine explained that there are three components to the human information system.

The simplest of these mechanisms is the reptilian brain. This device ensures that autonomic systems are operational. The heart beats, the body breathes, food is digested. The next level up is mammalian brain. This element is likely the most important in that it operates survival on a prehuman level of existence. A form of arousal, known now as emotion, developed and gave the mammal an edge over more primitive life.

Beyond the mammalian brain is the cortex, the human brain. This upper-level structure allows us to analyze, to reason, and to be creative. This structure is the home of verbalization, thinking, problem solving, and learning.

Figure 3.1 StressFire originator Massad Ayoob shows his aggressive isosceles stance during a firearms media new product roll-out of the Beretta Px4 pistol. Arms are straight and locked; the grip is a crush grip. His shoulders are ahead of his waist and his stance is open.

The amygdala resides in the mammalian brain and is the home of the "fight or flight" response, the body's alarm reaction.

Some object to the "fight or flight" moniker because we observe a few other possible responses. One other is "freeze." At first glance, this seems to be a mostly human innovation. Does the amygdala lack sufficient operating ability in this subject? If so, that could account for the "freeze" response in a couple of ways.

First, it could simply not work and make the reptilian response of immobility the response tactic of choice. Many predators have poor eyesight and require the prey's movement to find them. If the prey "freezes," perhaps the predator will be unable to find it and go in search of a less developed critter.

On the other hand, the "freeze" could occur because the amygdala could not shut the cortex off. This allows alternatives, choices, and rational process—something slow enough to ensure your demise. Or panic, a sensory overload, could set in. Or the prey could just give up.

The fourth "f" in our "fight, flight, or freeze" compilation won't be expressed in the "f" format. Suffice to say, it involves sexual arousal. Under extreme battle conditions, more than one combatant has experienced sexual arousal. In fact, the dead have shown some physical evidence of having had the same response.

While there may be data to support an explanatory model, I'm not aware of any. It does make for some concern in combatants who have this response. I can only explain that it does happen and there's no evidence to sustain a mental illness diagnosis. The same path in our brains is used by hormones for battle arousal and for sexual arousal, which helps to rule out the mental health issue.

Symptoms

If you've never been in a fight, the physiopsychological aspects can be stunning indeed. A single individual may experience some of these symptoms and not others. It seems that no two people have the same experience.

Many report that their perceptions of time and space are skewed. Some report that "time slows down." It's like everything is in slow motion. Others say, "It happened so fast!" Called "tachypsychia"—the "speed of the mind"—it has to do with a perception of time being slowed down or speeded up. This can be a problem when the time to report what happened arrives.

Another perceptual disorder is the distortion of vision and hearing. It's strange to hear an officer report that his duty sidearm sounded like a cap pistol discharging—while the offender's gun put out a blast like the deck gun from the *U.S.S. Missouri.* A number of officers, shot on their body armor, reported they heard no shot fired; they only saw the gun discharge and felt an impact.

Some see only the immediate threat. Officers who've interviewed store clerks who'd been robbed are often told that the suspect's gun was huge—with a muzzle that looked like a tunnel. Often, these guns turn out to be small caliber handguns or sawn-off .22 rifles.

Figure 3.2 StressFire presumes stress. The starting signal for this stage of fire was the application of a charge from a stun gun to the shooter. The instructor is Mas Ayoob; the student is the author.

The officers who have this perceptual narrowing often report seeing the armed offender and are surprised to find out that he was between two other people the officer never saw!

There are more symptoms, and the smart firearms instructor learns about them and what causes them. The ones listed are odd enough. These reactions, put together with cops who are surprised that someone is trying to kill them, and overlay that with the need for shooting skill, and it is no surprise that a confusing picture emerges.

Mastery

What is needed to fire an accurate shot? Strictly speaking, it's grip, sight alignment–sight picture, trigger control, and follow through. Although there are other elements, that's all you must have to fire an accurate shot.

Now boost your blood pressure from 120/80 to 220/190, your pulse to around 90 or 100, dilate your eyes, and involuntarily evacuate waste materials while you try to grip your firearm, get a good alignment of the sights over the threat, practice smooth trigger control, and follow through. Is that likely?

With StressFire, it can be. The grip is the "hammerfist" crush grip on the handgun. The eyes look over the gun at the threat, with the top of the slide

Figure 3.3 The aggressive forward lean of the StressFire isosceles is extended to the kneeling position, as Ayoob shows here.

looking much like a runway aimed at the suspect. The gun is aligned between your eyes. The hard grip makes it nearly impossible to jerk the trigger.

The pistol needs to be in front of your face. Although you may *soften* focus on the front sight, you have to have the pistol superimposed onto the target. In StressFire, the shooters work with the Weaver stance of the modern technique and then with a major derivative, the Chapman modification of the Weaver. Finally, StressFire practitioners shoot with the aggressive isosceles position that Ayoob prefers.

In shooting around the clock—360 degrees—you can find yourself twisted into a Weaver or a reverse Weaver. The bottom line is that StressFire is more about grip and vision than about stance. The idea is to master all of the major stances, as they feed into the different positions in which a shooter may find himself or herself.

Again, the Weaver stance is based upon isometric resistance. The handgun is pushed forward with the gun hand while the other hand presses back. The arms may or may not be locked—there are people who cannot lock the elbows or who have "tennis elbow," precluding the locked arm technique. With the Chapman modification, the gun arm is straight and locked, the bicep is cheeked like a rifle stock. Isometric tension is maintained, pressing out while pulling back. This is a very precise shooting platform with the potential for quite a bit of speed.

Isosceles is, as the name implies, a triangular formation—both arms extended (locked or not), with the shoulder line forming the triangle's base. I've seen the "loose" isosceles where both arms are bent somewhat but still equal. If one adds dynamic, isometric tension with the shooting hand pushing and the non-gun hand pulling, we're back to a Weaver—though it doesn't look like one from the outside.

Figure 3.4 The shooter on the left is in a classic Weaver stance. The shooter in the center is shooting an aggressive isosceles.

The stress one would normally expect from a sudden deadly threat feeds into the techniques, each of them designed to hold a small, light firearm very still while rolling a trigger back.

Firearms operation is a complex motor skill. In an attempt to find the Holy Grail, Ayoob has worked to find a way to use the stress that destroys the

Figure 3.5 This view shows use of the sights. Using the silhouette of the gun, looking at it from the rear, the slide can be used to point the gun. If the target is optically wider than the slide of the pistol, control the trigger to make the hit.

Figure 3.6 While the stance isn't open, it's a strong isosceles. The following figures are sequence shots of recoil effective from this very stance.

fine dexterity that is needed to hold the gun against tremors, shaking, and recoil and to put those bullets into the mark when needed.

The U.S. Army thought so much of the program they made it standard.

Instinct

Ever hear about or read about "instinct" shooting? It doesn't exist, strictly speaking. How about "point shooting"? It seems to me that everyone points and shoots. It's a matter of degrees.

Once upon a time (1907), a British citizen went to the English territorial possession of Shanghai in China to be a policeman. A British Marine, William Ewart Fairbairn, got deeply involved in the unarmed combat scene and developed a system of hand-to-hand combat. Over the years, he became an armed combat specialist as well, using a simple "point-and-fire" technique to teach the Shanghai Municipal Police the techniques consistent with the threat they faced in the street—as opposed to a stationary, dueling type of training.

As the decades passed and the conflict to be remembered as World War II loomed, Fairbairn was called back to train British, and eventually American, troops to use his methods. As you consider live fire houses in the current

Figure 3.7 The first shot has broken. The sights are aligned on the target while the empty cartridge case is barely away from the gun.

Figure 3.8 The second shot is the same as the first, the empty cartridge case just above the gun.

Figure 3.9 The third shot was photographed as the shot broke: the gun is at maximum recoil, the slide is back at full extension, and the brass has barely cleared the ejection port. The gun is the powerful Glock 37 chambered for the new .45 GAP cartridge.

era, remember that Fairbairn's "House of Horrors" predated the shoot house of today by 50 years!

He gained a disciple, Rex Applegate, in the United States. Colonel Applegate was no slouch before Fairbairn got a hold of him. He was even better after the exposure. They both preached a point shooting method that is easily taught, trained in a short period of time, and still in use today.

It begins with a compulsive grip. Like StressFire, which followed it, the technique flows around the hard grip. At close ranges, the straightened arm is raised like a pump handle until the gun comes into peripheral view. The trigger is rolled back as the gun stops on target center.

While I've heard it said that the modern technique trainers would never have anything to do with such heresy, one revealed to me that it was the technique of choice for him to teach in one situation. A man had come to him and said that his wife was threatened by a former spouse. She was a professional woman who didn't care for the idea of firearms and would train exactly one hour—reluctantly. If she couldn't get good enough to face her demise with that level of training, she wouldn't even waste that short amount of time.

Our trainer agreed to take her on. He selected the Ruger Standard .22 auto. She'd have no time to learn recoil control or precision shooting, let alone learn to deal with the blast of centerfire cartridges. He used standard

Figure 3.10 Gun expert Ed Lovette demonstrates the ready position of the current iteration of the Applegate point shooting technique. Interestingly, the crush grip of StressFire came from Applegate's point shooting method.

typing paper as targets and used just enough ammo to teach her to raise her arm and fire. She quickly got to the point that she hit the target repeatedly.

After a discussion of mind-set, she was sent on her way. He found out later that the situation was resolved without the use of gunfire on her part. "All we had time for was Applegate," he told me later. "And I have no doubt, she would have prevailed."

Figure 3.11 Lovette has the gun up ready to fire. His non-gun arm is up to block any attempt to strike him. Point shooting is normally done at close range.

Figure 3.12 This shooter is point shooting. Look at the distance between the slide of the pistol and his line of sight.

Figure 3.13 Same shooter, one handed. The gun is below his line of sight.

Figure 3.14 The gun is about chin level. An examination of his targets showed good hits.

Figure 3.15 Jim Cirillo is shown here at a law enforcement seminar explaining why he felt the need for his "alternative sighting techniques" even though he used traditional shooting technique—utilizing the sights—in his first shootout.

Alternative Sighting Methods

No less a subject matter expert than the late Jim Cirillo sat in on a panel discussion I moderated for the 11th annual International Training Seminar of the American Society of Law Enforcement Trainers in Mobile, Alabama, in January 1998. That panel discussed point shooting.

Using equipment supplied by Beamhit, Jim demonstrated his alternative sighting techniques. The "weapon silhouette" is remarkably like the Stress-Fire point index except that Jim didn't look over the gun. He covered the target looking through the slide while ensuring that the gun was perfectly level relative to the target. All you do then is control the trigger.

His other alternative was the nose point. Holding the gun centered on your body below your line of sight and pointing straight to your front, the gun is lined up with one thing that is centered between your eyes—your nose. Keeping everything in relative alignment, you turn like a turret and stop when aligned with the threat.

Jim was known for using his sights in a famous New York City bodega gunfight against three armed robbery suspects. He said that he'd seen his front sight so clearly that he saw minor imperfections in the front sight blade. During a break, a member of the panel's audience asked me to ask Jim a question: if he'd seen his sights so clearly when he shot it out with three gunmen, why was there a need for alternative sighting techniques?

After the break, in front of a full audience, I asked Jim why we needed alternatives when sights worked fine for him in his first gunfight.

"Well, it wasn't a normal gunfight," he said. "I had good lighting, I had distance between me and the perpetrators, I had what I thought was cover, and I had time. I'd known they were there and that I was going to have to face them. I wasn't surprised."

He went on, "Most gunfights are 'step around the corner and there it is.' It's dark, there's no cover, and you're up close. That's when you need something else."

Fairbairn and Applegate couldn't have said it any better.

Figure 3.16 Sometimes you are so close you can't bring the gun in front of your body without putting it in reach of your attacker. In that case, you have to be able to make hits "from retention" or from the hip.

Figure 3.17 This shooter has the gun out in front, defeating the purpose.

Figure 3.18 At this distance, the attacker can lunge and grab the front of the pistol. Note the brass just starting to leave the ejection port.

Issues of Teaching and Learning for Adults

4

Learning Styles, Teaching Styles

This chapter is the all-too-short culmination of my investigation into methods of instruction, which began in about 1969. I was a high school student and I recall starting to notice the difference in the styles of various teachers to whom I was exposed. I saw the virtual continuum between laissez-faire "babysitters" and doctrinaire practitioners; between those who would read to students from the slide on the overhead projector to those who would engage students, arouse curiosity, and demand achievement. As a youth, I was surprised at the differences that were allowed. Wasn't there one true way to teach? Or to learn?

Others had to see this and wonder. As I've gone through life involved in various capers, I return to the origin—and the origin is teaching, passing it on to the group that follows. It's part of keeping them safe while gaining proficiency so they can pass their lessons on to those who follow them. And on it goes, as long as the race lasts.

Figure 4.1 Discussion lecture is often informal and takes place between shooting drills on the range.

G.I. Beans

Our high school had just opened, adding to the previous high school in our town and making both institutions 4-year schools for the first time. Junior high was reduced to 2 years. We had the option of enrolling in Army Reserve Officer Training Corps. I took that option.

During the first year, the training corps was somewhat disorganized. The second year saw the arrival of Sergeant First Class (SFC) Don Bowling, late of the Pacific Campaign and owner of two artificial kneecaps. He was a driven individual and he expected everyone around him to be driven as well.

SFC Bowling was the kind of instructor who always talked about becoming the best and about the personal responsibility inherent in every human activity. He organized the drill team, a drum and bugle corps, and a constantly operational color guard, among other things. He had us doing fund drives to accumulate the cash for various functions off campus and to fund the annual Military Ball. We had the annual General Inspection to prepare for. It was a busy time.

A number of us flourished during this period—no surprise based on the quality of Bowling's leadership. He was simply superb. He wasn't perfect; he displayed a few dismaying tendencies—very few—but his overall tenure at the institution was reflected by the trophies won and the qualities of the lives his students led.

Because the beginning of the program was somewhat disjointed, we had more seniors than we had staff positions during my last year. Bowling saw that coming and instituted the Assistant Instructor (AI) program. He was the sole instructor of a program that likely exceeded 100 students. He needed help, and help was there for the taking.

The program actually began late in the spring preceding the fall term when we would start our instructional duties. Then, and during the summer, the AI candidates took our classes in methods of instruction. This was a very formal program, Army all the way, and our instructional materials were marked with the logo of the U.S. Army Infantry School, Ft. Benning, Georgia. Very doctrinaire in style, all instructors had to be the same in every vital area. The responsibility for learning was on the instructor. The failure of the student was the failure of the instructor to teach or to motivate learning. Lecture was a structured activity, handled a specific way. Although it may not sound that way in the current era, much of the material was a reflection of adult learning theory.

What follows is my admittedly imperfect recollection of the Army way of the era. I was asked by a reader if I insisted that instructors all use "the Way." Like everything else in this book, it is "a way," not "the Way." Learn from it, take what fits, and leave that which doesn't. Have someone else watch and evaluate your presentations.

Methods 101

The instructor marches in to the lectern. This device is handy for storing notes, chalk (this predates the whiteboard), the instructor's watch, keys, and pocket change. You never have anything in your pockets and you certainly don't "jingle" the change in your pocket during a lecture.

We went so far as to remove the clock above the blackboard in front of the room and put it in back. The clock is there to ensure that the instructor is on schedule, not to distract students.

The instructor doesn't use the lectern for "cover." It is a place to check in periodically, to ensure you're following the lesson plan. The instructor makes eye contact, all the time and with every student. The instructor walks in "Vs" and "Ws" so that his or her back is never turned to the students. Imagine a corner at the back of the stage. The instructor walks forward toward the center of the stage and the student-audience while speaking. He or she then backs away diagonally to complete the "V." The "W" starts out at a front corner, backs at an angle, facing the students. One may turn to write on the board, but one *never* speaks while doing so. It's rude and some of us are hard of hearing. Then the instructor comes forward to center stage, completing the move by backing—then forward again. Give the students' eyes a moving target. Make them track you.

Remember leaving your watch at the lectern? If your classroom has no clock, you sneak a peek at the watch while checking your progress against the lesson plan. Everything we do, our sole and total objective, is to minimize distractions and maximize the opportunity to learn.

"For the next thirty minutes, we will explore the cycle of function of the 7.62 mm rifle." That is a standard introduction to the block of instruction. It's followed by the body of the lesson.

"For the past thirty minutes, we learned the cycle of function of the M14 rifle. Are there any questions?" That ends the lesson.

Therefore, we tell them *what* we are going to teach. We then teach, *telling* them. That's followed by telling them what we *told* them. They get it three times. How do you tell them?

"Keep it simple," SFC Bowling said. "Write it on toilet paper, so they can see through it."

Figure 4.2 Gunsite rangemaster Ed Stock does a lecture-demonstration section in the classroom. Notice his trigger finger is off the trigger and on the frame. He's showing the right way to hold a magazine in his left hand.

Drill

Obviously, teaching close order drill (that is, marching) is not best done by the lecture approach. Much of what firearms instructors teach cannot be done by lecture.

The Army way includes "step-by-step," "talk-through," and "by the numbers." I've seen each of those used in firearms and, by the way, defensive tactics. Those who can't recall an example of the "by the numbers" method (used when the movement requires two or more counts) didn't study under Jeff Cooper. He used the five-count draw: grip-clear-click-smack-look (press). When the number was called, the trainees would execute that move—and that move only—and then await the next number to be called. As proficiency was gained, some numbers dropped out. This happens as fluidity appears.

Figure 4.3 Having put the loaded magazine in the gun, Ed is chambering a round. His trigger finger is still on frame.

Explanation and demonstration occur simultaneously in step-by-step as each element, or step, appears. The talk-through has a demonstrator doing a technique as the instructor narrates.

There is overlap. We can explain the presentation to threat, or draw and point, by the numbers, by step-by-step, and by talk-through. It depends on the audience and the environment.

Drill is repetitive exercise of a skill or technique. The School Drill is a student demonstration of skill level achieved in training. One problem is fatigue and another is the onset of boredom. Learning stops when the brain is no longer engaged due to either issue. Whether you have 5 students or 30, a few need continued repetition beyond what the remainder need. If the entire group or relay is held back with the slower achieving students, fatigue and boredom are issues. If the more advanced are moved on while the slower group works to keep up, frustration and desperation set in.

Figure 4.4 Having cleared the gun, Ed Stock physically inspects the chamber. Modeling expected behavior is a tenet of adult education.

The Way of the Gun

To get the message across to adult learners, you have to (1) treat them like adults, (2) show them the relevance of the message, and (3) let them have some fun.

Dealing with (1) is simple: make each individual responsible. If you, the instructor, are the only one on the premises responsible for everyone's safety, you have no time to teach. Likewise, having the responsibility for motivating everyone is a full-time-plus job. Treating students as adults gives them the chance to act like adults. They will act responsibly if given the opportunity.

These are people you are going to expect to operate safely and responsibly when on the street, in public, and wearing and handling guns. It defies belief that you would trust them with firearms in their homes, in our neighborhoods, in our public offices, in our stores and hospitals, but not trust them with firearms on the range. You have to start trusting them sometime. It stands to reason that the time to start is on the range where the opportunity for tragedy is so much smaller.

Figure 4.5 Stock has let the slide go into battery on the presumably cleared gun. Muzzle is still directed away from people and finger is away from trigger.

How many times have you entered firing range property and seen the signs "No loaded weapons beyond this point"? The question presents that, if loaded guns are not allowed on the premises, is it then illegal to shoot on those premises? Firearms won't shoot if empty.

A better rule is Shepherd's Prime Directive: All handguns will be holstered and all long guns will stay slung, unless directed by an instructor or coach. Who enforces such a rule? Everyone on the premises is responsible—the instructor *and* every student.

If your officers are responsible for public safety in your community, they can be responsible for officer safety on the range. Hold them to that responsibility. Anyone has the authority to call a "Cease fire!" at any time. When that happens, everyone freezes and no one does anything. Instructor personnel then search for the issue that required the cease fire and resolve the problem.

Similarly, if a trainee is uncertain of the condition of his or her holstered handgun, he or she can grab an instructor or another student to act as coach and advise that individual of the problem. Any coach or instructor can take

Figure 4.6 Notice that Ed puts his hand centered on his abdomen while reholstering—preventing his non-gun hand from getting around the muzzle. The gun goes back into the holster exactly opposite from the way it came out.

the student to a safe backstop and allow a condition check of the piece. The coach gets an additional learning opportunity by supervising gun handling.

Sometimes, the best way to learn is to have to teach.

"Why?"

It seems that the "why?" of a learning objective is as important as the content. The "why?" is the gateway to the student. It's the door through which adult education occurs. If anyone thinks that children will drive an adult to distraction by asking "why," he or she has never taught adult learners.

If I tell basic trainees that they have to have a grip high on the backstrap of the handgun, we'll spend a considerable amount of time going student to student fixing their low grips on handguns. Telling seldom seems to get it across. We can tell and show and do it again, but 30–50% of a basic class will need on-the-line remediation.

Figure 4.7 Training venues are often rough and lack amenities. Clive Shepherd uses lecture discussion and dry demonstration in an open area adjacent to the range.

On the other hand, if I explain grip and its relation to the cycle of operation of the semiauto handgun, I'll get a few more converts before we go "hands on." If I explain grip and cycle of operation and go on to explain and demonstrate how well recoil is handled for quick follow-up shots, I gain a few more.

Finally, if we go through all that and I go on to explain that gunfire seldom stops a determined attack—therefore, more shooting is necessary to get the offender to get down and stop shooting—then 70–85% or so will get it right the first time.

It doesn't take too long to explain the "whys" to adult learners. I insist that adult students take some responsibility for their own motivation, but I refuse to close any doors. If I'm telling you to do something, I have the duty to tell you why you need to do it.

Good Times

Adult learners seem to "get it" better and quicker when they enjoy their time in training. It seems that we always had people who dreaded training and coming to the range. Sometimes, the instructors are the reason.

We do joke around. Some of the humor gets rough and sometimes trainees get their feelings hurt. Do you think they want to learn something from you if you hurt their feelings? This is something that hits close to home. In all my years of instruction, I've had few complaints. In each of those cases, someone had gotten his or her feelings hurt. How does that make me feel?

Figure 4.8 Learning by the numbers: Gunsite operations manager Ed Head demonstrates step 1 of the five-count draw (grip).

The responsibility for teaching rests with me, and my ultimate goal is to get the message across to the student. Sometimes feelings do get hurt—but if you can't run your pistol during a firefight, don't try to talk your killer out of taking you. He doesn't care. If your pistol stops shooting during a fight, you

Figure 4.9 Sometimes it takes two: a pair of instructors share demo (left, with cast aluminum training gun) and lecture.

Figure 4.10 Use of a demonstrator and a nonfiring training gun lets students see (visual) a person modeling the behavior (allowing kinesthetic understanding) while a lecturer discusses each element (auditory learning).

Figure 4.11 Insufficient drill forces students to have to look to do simple tasks. This shooter has to look at the gun to reload.

won't be able to put your hand up, waiting for an instructor to fix it; you're too late. Don't cry to me.

Imagine this scenario. A student has a target with an even distribution of bullet holes in every quadrant of the paper. There is no central cluster, there's just an even spread over the length of the paper. An instructor walks up to the student, makes sure the area forward (toward the impact berm) is clear,

Figure 4.12 Often all we need is to take the ear protection off to make a point while on the range.

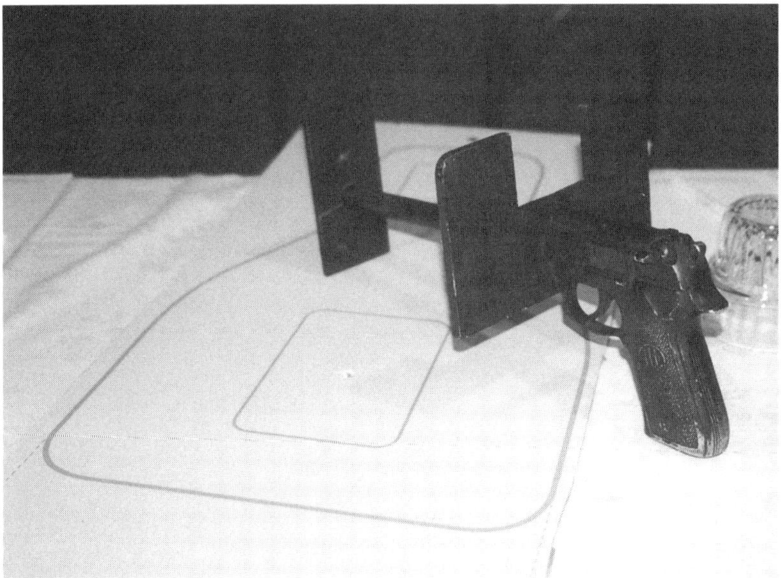

Figure 4.13 Visual aids are helpful. Want to show sight picture–sight alignment? A training gun with huge "sights" helps demonstrate the point.

and asks the student to get his or her pistol out and point it at the berm. He points at the bump on the front top of the slide.

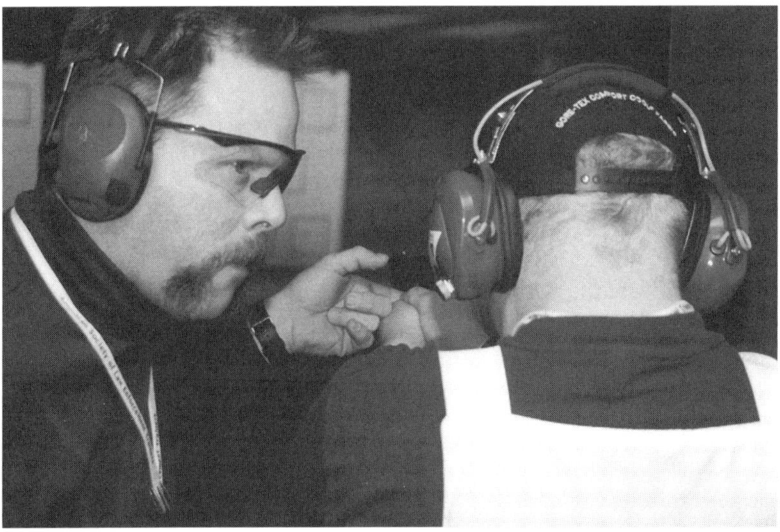

Figure 4.14 Master instructor Peter Burlingame does the exemplar drill—he runs the trigger for the shooter, reinforcing issues of arc of movement and surprise break.

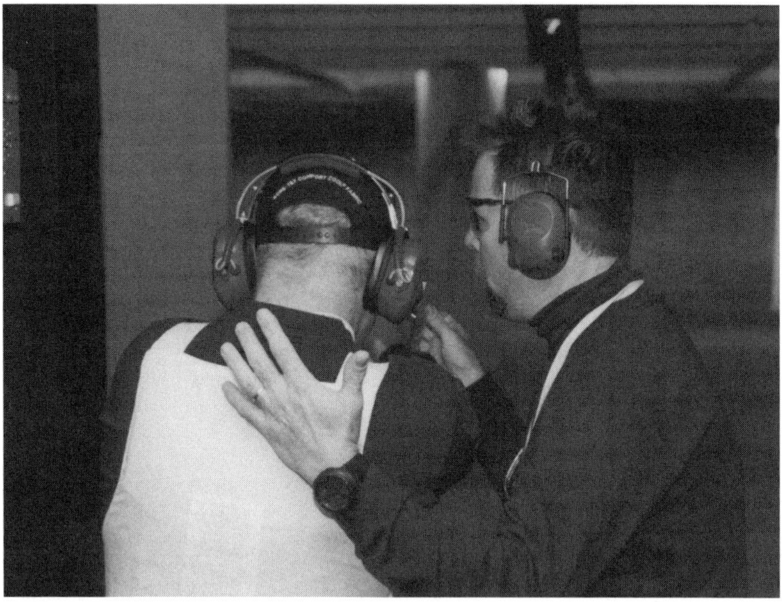

Figure 4.15 Standing next to the shooter gives more visual information. The coach is pulling the trigger for the student.

"See that?" he asks sarcastically. "That, right there." He taps the front sight with his index finger.

"It's the front sight. Someone went to a lot of time, trouble, and expense to put that on there. Think we ought to use it once in a while there, Sunshine?"

Meanwhile every other student on the range sees and hears the exchange. What are they thinking? "Next time, that could be me."

Before a reader thinks I'm casting aspersions on the instructor in our hypothetical example, think again. I understand his frustration. I've been there. You try and try and try again. Frankly, some people just won't get the Deal. Skill with firearms won't happen for those individuals. I've known people who have gone through entire careers, who have gotten to the top of the profession, and who should never have carried a gun in public. That said, I've also known people who got instructor certified who didn't know a stock screw bushing from a barrel bushing.

My understanding aside, if we're going to reach a maximum number of the untrained, we have to try to get them to have a little fun and at the same time understand the serious context of the training. It can be a fine line.

One method of increasing the fun factor is to use competition—sparingly—to reinforce training points while simultaneously driving up pressure on student performance—without judgment—and getting them to work as a team.

Figure 4.16 Competition helps teach lessons and is an acceptable use of pressure in training.

I did an instructor seminar class in Texas and incorporated some competition on the steel target range they had between their two square ranges. We had an even number of Pepper Poppers (steel knock-down targets) on each side and had two lines of students. It was a simple shooter-against-shooter elimination to get to the "fastest, most accurate" shooter in class.

They quickly understood that running such an exercise a hundred times with the same group would give each student a "win." Such events are mostly to reinforce training points and to blow off a little steam.

In one shoot-off, the shooter on the right mowed his targets down while his partner struggled with a stoppage. The shooter on the right, having cleared his targets, said, "I'll cover you!" and shot the other competitor's targets down.

The student with the stoppage was somewhat deflated, but the opportunity to reinforce team tactics and the need for looking after our partners emerged. On his next run, his pistol ran without difficulty and he knocked down his opponent/partner's last target!

Summing Up

Teaching and learning takes up volumes and makes up entire degree programs in institutions of higher learning. All that can't be explained here. For

Figure 4.17 Breaking a class down into two relays (coach and pupil) helps everyone learn everything twice. The shooter is shooting from retention and his coach is modeling the behavior as he watches.

purposes of this seminar-like book, we can only give a thumbnail sketch and a few things to think about.

For example, adult learners come in three basic varieties: visual, auditory, and kinesthetic. Most of our students are a mix of the three with a strong preference for one input method over the others. To hedge our bets, we try to teach everything we can in a manner to reach visual ("I can see your point"), auditory ("I hear you"), and kinesthetic (actually moving while watching a demonstration) learners. It's not easy and it takes practice.

While I had a heavy teaching load—in-service and prep classes for recruits at the department, adjunct teaching at a university, and doing seminars for instructor groups—I was a junkie for televangelists. I would watch every chance I had, not for content that could actually be beneficial for my character but for their style, methods, inflections, and mannerisms. I would reject what didn't fit my persona and adopt what fit. I would do anything I could to reach my audience. I felt that the content of my classes was important—for in-service and basic classes, the material could have life-saving import—and that anything I could do to get my message out, I should do.

That concern also appeared in live-fire training. I didn't ask students to perform a skill I hadn't already shown them in live fire. We demonstrated drills, exercises, the skills they had to demonstrate, and even did an exemplar

Safety, Part I

5

Safety is the responsibility of the individual. If one ever enters onto a firing range or accepts the accountability inherent in the ownership of firearms, the first thing to be considered is that safety is everyone's duty. (The same is true of automobiles.)

That is so important that it needs to be posted. It needs to appear on the walls of the building, classroom, and range—"All personnel are assigned to duty as Safety Officers—Safety is *everyone's* responsibility."

Only a few years ago range training was conducted as if all the students were going to compete in Police Pistol Combat (PPC) or bull's-eye types of matches. It wasn't apparent that anyone was there to learn how to win a gunfight. Ranges were run one way only, and this was before the distinctions between "cold" and "hot" ranges were even named. Only one way was safe.

The shooters came to the line with empty guns. They stood still on the line; no movement was allowed. They all loaded at the same time, fired the same number of shots, and shot the same way. They ran empty at the same time and reloaded when told.

Shooters had to be told before they could do anything. It was Jeff Cooper who ran it the other way round: all guns were loaded. (Consider this: if you are on patrol and report to the range, where are you supposed to unload to be "safe"? Why is the gun "safe" at the range when unloaded, but not unsafe on the street while it's loaded?)

The only way any gun could be unloaded is "Make ready for dry practice." Otherwise, the piece should be ready for battle. Carrying a loaded gun on a firing range is appropriate—where else can one learn safe handling of loaded guns? Range safety is artificial. We teach specific techniques and attempt to get quantifiable results. The street isn't so clean. The offender moves, the officer moves. Cover is where you find it, not where you put it. The light is broadly variable and uncontrolled.

The presumption that every gun is always loaded assures appropriate handling of the piece. If someone asks whether a gun is loaded, the officer had best know the answer—what good is it empty? Unloaded is a temporary and hazardous condition—hazardous because "unloaded" has been taken to mean "safe." Nothing can be further from the truth.

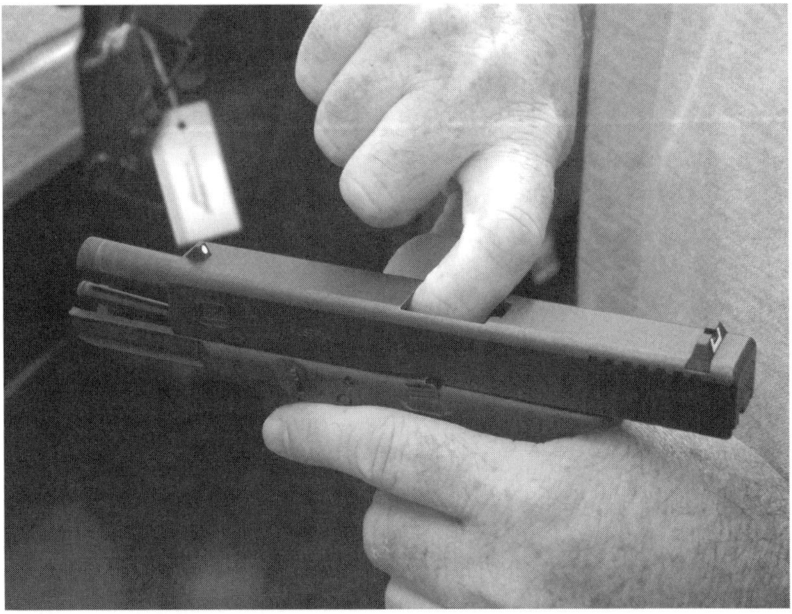

Figure 5.1 Checking firearms for condition means to lock them open and check visually (look into the chamber) and physically (insert a finger into the chamber, feeling for a cartridge). The pistol is a Glock.

Four Main Safety Rules

I've been to a facility where range safety was considered so important that it consumed two thick volumes of text. The books explicitly laid out every possible situation and explained every appropriate response. While it wasn't as voluminous as the federal tax code, it was as complex and cumbersome.

Rules that are verbose tend to be ignored because they can't be understood. Our shooters aren't stupid people and can't be treated as if they are. There are four rules, the primary rules, that govern all conduct with firearms—at the range, at home, at the station, at the hospital, or at a shopping mall, in training or in operational activities. Espoused by Jeff Cooper, posted at Gunsite, and copied in every book on the subject there is—in one or another form—they are universally accepted and must be ingrained in the user.

Rule #1: *All guns are always loaded.* This is not a fantasy. There are those who point out that the statement is untrue as written. All guns, they argue, have to be unloaded sometimes. That presupposes that unloaded guns are *safe*. That is crap.

Gun accidents are nearly always followed with the exclamation, "It was *unloaded!*" It seems the empty ones are the problem. So, none are empty. Ever. They are always handled with the respect given a loaded gun.

Figure 5.2 Demonstrations in front of a class can be done "empty-handed." Some instructors refer to the "finger gun," but making light of the technique ignores its utility and safety.

Be careful when you are around the uninformed. I once had to take firearms to a professional photographer. This individual isn't a gun person. In fact, most gun persons aren't really familiar with the four rules. I had the opportunity, the day before writing this chapter, to have this photographer point a Kel-Tec P32 auto at me, finger on the trigger, as he explained a point.

I know, it was *just* a .32 auto—but none of us wants to get shot, not even with a small caliber handgun.

Someone will ask, "Was it loaded?" My response is, "Yes" (see Rule #1), but it really doesn't matter. It's the habit of assuming guns can be safe that's dangerous. Guns don't kill people; professional photographers do.

As instructors, we have to model the behavior we expect students to adopt. This means that we observe Rule #1 even when handling deactivated, demilled, nonfiring guns or replica guns. Remember, it's the habit that kills or doesn't kill.

Simulations require special safety handling, which is discussed in Chapter 11. In that exercise, guns (models that shoot marking cartridges or "Airsoft" guns with pellets) are often aimed at and shot at other people—role-players and the like—but that requires a mind-set change going in and rehabilitation coming out.

In life, generally, Rule #1 controls.

Rule #2 is often stated as, "*Don't allow the muzzle to cover anything you don't intend to destroy.*" I prefer that we direct the muzzle in a safe direction at all times. Manny Kapelsohn, attorney and firearms instructor, attended a

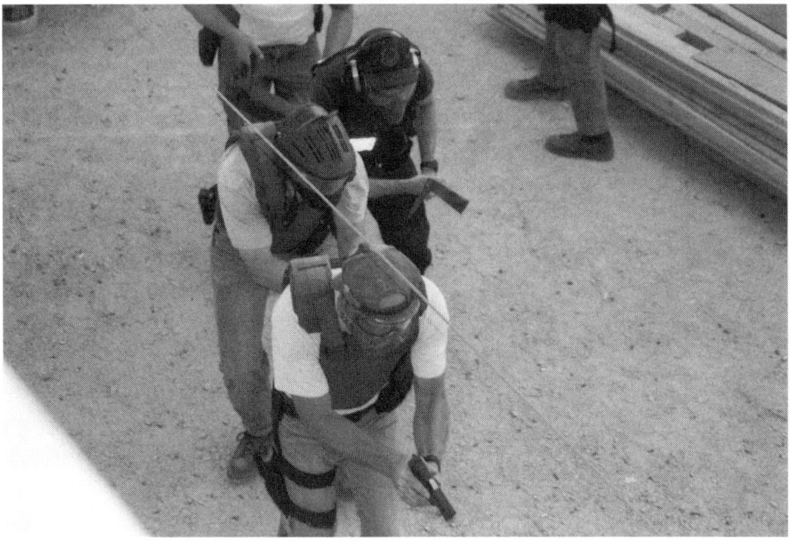

Figure 5.3 Muzzle direction is critical. Muzzles can't be directed at other persons unless we're engaged in shooting them.

class of mine at a conference of the now-defunct American Society of Law Enforcement Trainers.

His critique covered only my safety rules, particularly Rule #2. In light of his critique, my Rule #2 says "Keep the muzzle pointed in a safe direction at all times." What is a safe direction? A safe direction is one in which an unintended discharge can cause *no* personal injury and only minor property damage. If someone steps in front of the muzzle, the gunhandler is responsible for diverting the muzzle to the safest direction.

What about taking offenders at gunpoint? That has been argued long and eloquently on both sides. That said, I prefer to keep the muzzle in a *safe* direction.

Rule #3 is, "*Keep your finger off the trigger and out of the trigger guard until the muzzle is pointed at the target (threat) and the decision to fire has been reached.*" I've seen it put in crude and vulgar terms. I approve of anything that gets the message across. Rule #3 violations are among the most common and egregious safety violations. I've seen really good cops fail to observe it. I've seen target shooters and competition shooters violate it. I've seen tens of thousands of repetitions of people in violation of Rule #3, as everyone has, on television—in entertainment programs and the news—and in motion pictures.

We just didn't know better. We thought that we could put our foot on the accelerator without the car lurching forward. No one thought of the result of the startle effect or of a sudden loss of balance.

Hold an infant in both hands, arms extended overhead, and the baby will laugh as you do. But if you make a sudden sound, "Whoops!" and act like you are dropping the baby, his little eyes clamp shut as both of his hands ball into tight little fists. Now, if little Wilbur has a gun in hand, that little index finger, along with all the fingers and thumbs of both hands, will curl shut—and there will be a "bang!"

Keep your finger off the trigger until the muzzle is pointed at the target (threat) and you have formed the intention of firing.

Rule #4 is "*Be sure of your target, backstop, and beyond.*" Visually identify the target. Don't shoot at sounds if you can't see what's making the sound. Know what's behind the target (threat). Know what is on either side of it.

The four rules are not range rules. They're life rules, active and appropriate everywhere, all the time. The odd situation in simulations—role-play, or "reality-based" training—calls for a refinement of mind-set with absolute, rigidly enforced rules that exist in that world only. It requires a secure area, a disarming station manned by one individual who'll be present to check people in and out and to ensure that the training area is sterile.

Life is like that nowhere else.

The four rules otherwise control all training and operational needs as well as controlling everyday life.

Physical Safety Checks

Is it too much to expect people to accept the four rules, to know them by heart, and to live by them? They're simple enough and easily remembered and recited. We can still make mistakes, but we can make them without personal injury resulting.

The center rules, Rules #2 and #3, are the main physical safety checks. We can stand on a range—or watch the news reports depicting our troops in the "Sandbox"—and tell if Rule #2 and Rule #3 are being observed.

Rule #2—the safe direction or muzzle discipline rule—has to do with muzzle orientation. If the carbine is hanging, muzzle down, we consider that a safe direction—but don't let the muzzle cross your legs or feet!

"But what if the chamber's empty?" Refer to Rule #1.

This isn't about the operating condition of the piece, it's about the operating condition of the brain.

We can see, on the range, if the pistols are all pointed at the impact berm. We can see if the muzzle is down or, in fewer situations, pointed over the horizon.

Rule #2 is the first of the physical safety checks. The second is Rule #3. We can likewise look across the range and see that the fingers are (1) off the triggers, (2) out of the trigger guards, and (3) up on the frame.

Massad Ayoob likes for his people to have the index finger bent and up on the frame. That's good, though for some of us with weaker vision it's a problem. We see bent fingers and assume that the bent finger is on the trigger. For a number of other reasons, the bent index finger is smart money. The rigidly extended finger can snap back into the trigger guard with enough force to depress the trigger and light a primer. The bent finger drops into the guard vertically, lessening the chance of a premature blast.

Similarly, if someone jumps out and grabs at your nonholstered firearm, your straight finger can be trapped or the gun can be forced into the rigid index finger, hyperextending it.

The arched index finger flexes and is stronger for being bent. The chances of injury lessen.

If we follow the middle rules and enforce them by visually confirming these physical safety checks, we vastly lessen the chances of a tragedy. Our almost religious adherence to them reinforces our belief that the firearm is loaded and makes us look hard to identify that threat before firing. They support Rules #1 and #4.

The physical safety checks are not "range-safety rules." They are life-safety rules. They govern all conduct of armed persons everywhere and at all times.

Safety Circle

A safety circle does not mean that anything you do in that circle is safe; it is not a "ready" position for the switched on. It is a product of having mind-numbed citizens, "lookie-Lou's" who have to see the train wreck. The safety circle is a place to "paint" the muzzle of the gun so as not to cover people who cross in front of your gun muzzle when you are aimed in at a threat.

I don't recommend walking in front of a line of shooters as they fire. I imagine that it is exhilarating in some ways, but can be considered foolhardy even if you know and trust them and their trainers. There is something reassuring about seeing muzzles dip to the safety circle as someone approaches the danger zone. That's why we have the safety circle.

Rule #2 is the "safest direction" rule. On the range, where is a safe direction? The safe direction is gun muzzles pointed at the impact berm. Everyone is told, "Keep the muzzles downrange." Downrange is pointed at the impact berm. Uprange is pointed at the instructor, spectators, automobiles, and a building or two.

Where is the safest direction at the shopping mall? At the station? At a residence? At your house? Can the walls of your house contain an unintentional

Figure 5.4 Clive Shepherd demonstrates his safety circle. Not a "ready position," it's a place to point the muzzle to prevent injury and property damage. The gun shown here is a toy, used for demonstration purposes.

Figure 5.5 The safety circle isn't static and stationary; one can move the gun as shown to redirect the muzzle without pointing it at other "no-shoots" in the area.

Figure 5.6 Clive is shown demonstrating and discussing the safety circle. It is simply a matter of rotating the wrist, pointing the muzzle down, and avoiding one's own feet.

discharge? It's unlikely. The bullet that breezes through drywall and siding could hit the kid on a bicycle outside.

Master trainer Clive G. Shepherd was a member of a Royal Marine commandos and served as a colour sergeant (CSgt). During his time in service, rifles were directed down at the deck when it was unsafe to point them out. Clive and his unit did some time during "the Troubles" in Northern Ireland. A place replete with "no-shoot targets," they had to find a place to point muzzles to minimize danger to the noncombatant population.

In his role as an instructor for concealed carry permit applicants and permit holders in South Florida, he used the wrist rotation technique to direct the muzzle to the deck when noncombatant people wandered into the midst of a problem. He taught that method to permit holders and later to police and police instructors.

It's Not a "Ready" Position

Guard or "ready" means the gun is in hand, the firing grip is attained, and the muzzle is directed below the target. It's that way because pointing over the horizon violates Rule #2 in most locales. In rare circumstances, a "muzzle high ready" could be required.

The safety circle is employed when there is a "no-shoot" who has intruded into the threat area. During an "active shooter" event when there is a team

Figure 5.7 Range exercises reinforce the safety circle. These students, armed with loaded handguns, are facing uprange—a safety violation on most ranges. They await the signal to fire.

member in front of you or when a nonshooting student appears, the muzzle has to be directed away from him or her.

The safety circle is an imaginary circle painted on the deck below your stance. The wider the stance, the wider the circle. If a shooter needs to check behind himself or herself, the gun can go too; if the safety circle is employed, the muzzle won't track around 180 degrees parallel to the deck. It'll be dialed in to the deck in a circle around the shooter's feet.

Consider that you're standing inside a large truck tire laid on the ground. The tire is the circle that is around your feet. That's where the muzzle goes. Simply rotate the wrist.

In a shooting scenario where the muzzle had to be directed down to avoid muzzling an innocent, the gun snaps back up and in line with the threat as the no-shoot passes the danger zone. It is very fast.

Figure 5.8 Having drawn into the safety circle, they begin the pivot downrange.

Figure 5.9 Now facing the threat, students proceed to engage them.

Cross-Draw Holsters Unsafe?

If you've ever attended or taught a class that warned prospective students that they wouldn't be allowed to use the cross-draw holsters, shoulder holsters, or fanny packs they actually use to carry the gun—because such holsters aren't safe on the range—then decision makers didn't understand the safety circle.

Are your officers allowed to use such holsters off the range? But if the holsters aren't safe to draw from on the range, how can they be safe on the street?

Figure 5.10 The "Conga line": Students with handguns in the safety circle move about the range—never violating Rule #2. Important to learn on the range, the safety circle is a technique critical to operational safety.

Figure 5.11 Likewise, the police shotgun (or carbine) can be put into a safe direction when someone wanders in front of a muzzle.

The safety circle is used to prevent muzzling bystanders when drawing from such holsters. Instead of showing the front of the gun to everyone in a 45-degree arc, direct the muzzle into the safety circle as it clears the holster. Snap the wrist locked as the muzzle lines up the center of the threat. It's safe for the range and on the street.

Figure 5.12 The shotgun is moved into the safety circle.

Figure 5.13 One student is still engaging a threat while his partner checks the surrounding area; his pistol is directed into the safety circle.

The four safety rules, the two main physical safety checks, and the safety circle are not simply range rules. They are a way of life. Take a class to ingrain the safety circle—check with NRA's law enforcement unit to take any of their instructor development schools. Last I heard, the safety circle is taught there.

Safety, Part II

6

Mat World

Although the term "mat world" has its roots in the defensive tactics class of police motor skills training, it's a good concept generally. It's long been commonly accepted that you learn nothing in school that is required in the "real" world. It takes the school of hard knocks—experience—to learn how to deal with life.

Mat world is school. We learn how to do techniques by the numbers. First, step here. Grasp there. Take your opponent's center. Pivot and bend. Take him down. We even mark the deck, as footwork isn't easy to learn for everyone. "It's more fun kissing when you know where the noses go."

As trainees "get the Deal," we push them to become more fluid, to flow, to do combinations. We want them to get comfortable. It's still mat world. There's the tap out rule—when the pain is too great, tap out on your partner, the mat, the wall.

There's the (possibly apocryphal) story of the peace officer who exerted control on an arrestee. The arrestee "tapped" out, the officer released, resulting in an escape attempt! That's taking mat world to the street.

Range-safety rules are in place for a reason: that's to keep everyone safe on the range (see Chapter 5). Do we need separate rules for the real world? Is range world so different? Concepts of hot and cold ranges bear closer examination.

Hot and Cold

As peace officers, we are expected to carry firearms that are loaded—rounds chambered—whenever we're out in the world. I've seen uniformed officers at residences, shopping malls, hospitals, schools, and post offices—and haven't seen people panic due to the presence of the presumably loaded gun. That same cop arrives at the range and he sees the sign: "Positively no loaded weapons are to be brought into this area!"

If he's safe in the citizens' homes, the mall, hospitals, schools, and postal facilities, why isn't he safe on the range with a loaded gun? It's because the officer comes to a shooting range expecting to shoot. That means that the mental restriction against pulling the gun from the holster is lifted, that he's got a predilection to touch the trigger. He knows he'll be shooting.

On a hot range, all guns are loaded. Periodically, you'll see a field-stripped handgun. We figure that because it's in pieces it's unloaded. That's likely to be true, but we remain wary.

The idea behind a cold range is that "Unloaded guns are safe." That's simply untrue; there's no such thing. On the cold range, all guns have to be unloaded except when a line is preparing to shoot. All those guns are "safe." So why do we have more gun accidents on cold ranges than hot ranges?

Safety isn't restricted to the range. We need for range world to be the same as real world. All guns are loaded. When drawn or unslung, all guns are pointed in a safe direction. We place a finger on the trigger when the muzzle is directed to the threat or target and we've formed the intention to fire. We visually identify the target, making sure of the threat, the "backstop," and beyond.

The Prime Directive

A range-world rule would be "All handguns stay holstered, all long guns stay slung, until called for by an instructor or coach." Real world is "common sense" and "good judgment."

Figure 6.1 Holstered sidearms are safe. They need to stay in the holster during range activities unless called for by instructor or coach.

Figure 6.2 On the range, long guns stay slung unless called for by instructor or coach.

By requiring an instructor or coach to be involved in decision making on the range, we deal with the "I knew that I'd be shooting when I came to the range" mind-set. Now we've increased the number of brains to be engaged before the gun is drawn or unslung. Two brains are pulled into the process, allowing the hot-range concept to reach its logical end.

If a student goes to another student and says, "I'm not sure my pistol's loaded and I need to check it," that other student will go along to a "fiddle" table or other safe direction and supervise the chamber/magazine check. The students are adults but only if treated as such.

I first ran across this range rule when I took a class from Clive Shepherd. He referred to this as the "Prime Directive." It is essential for any range activities.

Prime Directive: "All handguns stay holstered, all long guns stay slung, until called for by an instructor or coach."

Nonfiring Guns

Also known as training guns, nonfiring models are essential for use in an area where a "real" gun causes loss of learning due to accelerated heart rate

Figure 6.3 Which one is real? Feeling without looking, they are the same. When directed at another human being, the difference is profound. The red gun on the left is a nonfiring, factory-produced model used for demonstration. The center "blue" gun fires FX® marking cartridges. The one on the right is a Glock 22, chambered for the .40 S&W cartridge.

and increased blood pressure. Glock, Inc. sells a "red" gun analog of their famous firearms line. A conventional-looking Glock pistol, it has a red frame instead of a black or olive-drab (OD) green one. This red frame is to signify that there is no firing pin or firing pin channel in the slide and that the barrel is plugged. This should make it "safe."

The problem comes when a trainer moves from classroom to range and swaps the G22R red gun for the issue Glock 17 in his holster. While doing a demo on the range, the "real" gun comes out and a shot is unintentionally fired. The guns feel identical. Without looking, there's no way to tell what gun you have in the holster.

We've used cast guns made by Ring's Training guns and the smoothed over gun retention training guns—made of cast aluminum—by Lindell's Aluminum Training Guns. These do feel somewhat different. Not enough different, though, if you're doing a fast demo.

There've been a number of bad situations with "non-nonfiring" guns when we meant to use a nonfiring gun. The FBI Academy had an accidental shooting some years back when the instructor believed the demonstration gun was a nonfiring model. It's bad enough with guns used in simulations

Figure 6.4 Both of these guns—Glock and carbine—are set up to fire FX marking cartridges exclusively. They have to be tightly controlled and used in tightly controlled environments.

or reality-based (that is, non-mat-world mat-world) training, discussed later in the book.

The best way to approach the problem is to make everything the same all the time—as much as we can.

Preparation

To prepare for any gun work, we have to "make ready." The make-ready protocol should be used (1) when going onto duty, (2) when going to shoot on the range, (3) when preparing to do a demonstration in front of a class—or even one student, (4) when going out on private business when armed, and (5) when preparing to dry-fire—though with a different result.

Make ready is a standardized protocol with a few possible endings. One is "make ready holster." We make ready, we look and assess, and we holster and secure the sidearm. Another is "make ready guard." This is the make-ready procedure ending with the gun at "ready" or the guard position. "Make ready for a break," while range training, means to end up with the sidearm in the condition you need for it to be in to leave the range. After this procedure, some ranges want shooters to end up at "parade rest," with hands behind the back so instructors can tell who isn't ready. Other ranges want the gun

Figure 6.5 Making ready in stages. First, protect your eyes.

holstered and shooters facing uprange at the conclusion. "Make ready for dry practice" ends up with the gun and magazines empty and no ammo around them or you.

Make ready goes like this:

1. Protect your eyes and your ears.
2. Draw to guard.
3. Press check. Check the chamber (for loaded or empty), and check the magazines. If the gun is empty, load it. Continue with a "tac load," putting a fully loaded magazine in place of the one with the round down. At the conclusion of the process, you can load the "one-down" magazine with another cartridge.
4. Finish by going to guard, the holster or checked empty for dry practice.

Figure 6.6 Then protect your ears.

In the situation where the instructor goes to do a demonstration, the first thing to do is make ready. Students are watching. Let them see the drill. When they see you execute phase one (Protect your eyes, protect your ears), you may find them doing the same thing! The smart ones will.

Face the safest direction and continue with the make-ready process. When you draw to guard and press check, you can see that the Glock frame is red or that you are trying to ease the slide back on a cast aluminum gun. In either case, you can continue with the process. This is a quick way to teach make ready, but it has the safety benefit of giving you the chance to see which gun you have.

If it's real and loaded, let them see the unload process. They need visual repetitions of that as well.

Figure 6.7 Draw to guard in a safe direction and check the chamber.

If the handgun is stored in a lock box at home, I recommend the officer make ready before going on the road—or going out for a gallon of milk. The procedure is the same. Don't fail to protect your eyes and ears. Don't fail to point in to a safe direction.

Always make ready before doing a demonstration. Always, in every single case, go through the procedure. It'll pay dividends the first time you find that it's an M&P instead of a cast model.

Inherently Dangerous Instrumentalities

You'd believe that "inherently dangerous instrumentalities" would be a reference to any explosive materials, gas distribution systems, or electrical transmission lines. Some people would allege that firearms are inherently

Figure 6.8 Check the magazines for fully loaded condition.

dangerous instrumentalities, especially if children are exposed to them. Fatalities data don't support this conclusion.

In 2004, the Centers for Disease Control reported that there were 45,113 traffic deaths. In the same year, 29,569 fatalities resulting from firearms were reported.* Although 15,554 more people died from traffic-related causes in 2004, the Kansas Supreme Court didn't determine that motor vehicles were inherently dangerous instrumentalities, like dynamite, electrical transmission lines, or gas distribution systems…or firearms.

The Kansas Supreme Court determined that firearms are so dangerous they are analogous to dynamite. They didn't do this once, but twice. In both cases, hammer-headed teens took firearms belonging to their parents; in both cases, the firearms had been locked up. They were empty—remember, duffers

* Data for both are from http://webapp.cdc.gov/sasweb/ncipc/mortrate10_sy.html.

Figure 6.9 The press check is done close to the body using the non-gun hand over the back of the slide. The firing grip is compromised to physically check the chamber.

believe unloaded guns are safe. The teens took those guns and contrived to cause injury to other youngsters "by accident." When the cases made their way to the Supreme Court, the court decided that the defendants were to be held to a higher standard of care; whether the firearms were locked up or not, if those kids got to them they weren't locked up enough.

In *Long v. Turk*, 265 Kan. 855, 962 P.2d 1093 (1998), the question was whether the gun owners exercised the "highest degree of care" in securing firearms.

The court reports,

> The defendant's minor son, Matthew, was driving his car when he encountered the plaintiff's minor son, Tony, driving a van. Matthew and Tony shouted at each other while the vehicles drove side-by-side for a few blocks. Matthew eventually reached under the floor mat and pulled out his father's .357 Magnum handgun and fired one shot out the passenger side window. The hollow point slug went through the window of Tony's van, killing him.
>
> Matthew's father owned several guns which were kept in a locked safe, although Matthew knew where the keys were kept. A .357 Magnum and the hollow point bullets for the gun were kept in a gun cabinet. Testimony conflicted as to whether Matthew had permission to take the gun out of the locked cabinet. (Cited in *Wood v. Groh,* 269 Kan. 420, 7 P.3d 1163 [2000])

Since Matthew knew where the keys were, the fact that the gun was locked up didn't matter.

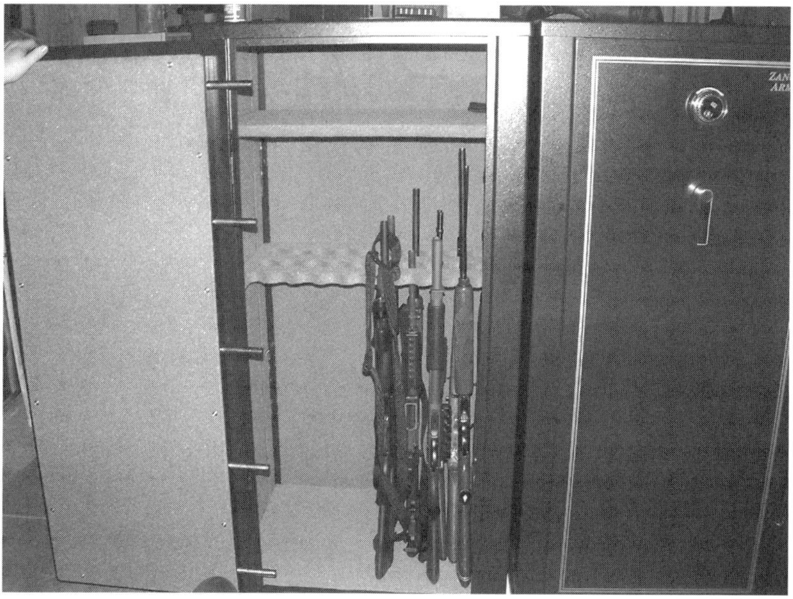

Figure 6.10 In some states, this is the only lawful way to store firearms—if the combination and key access are strictly controlled. Compare to the car keys left carelessly unsecured.

This case was followed in Kansas by *Wood v. Groh*, 269 Kan. 420, 7 P.3d 1163 (2000). In this case, a personal injury action was brought against a gun owner and his wife, after the gun owner's minor son accidentally shot the teenaged victim at a late-night party. The gun was kept locked up in a gun cabinet. The Kansas Supreme Court found that sufficient evidence existed to support instruction to the jury on negligent parental supervision because their son was easily able to break into the cabinet with a screwdriver.

The information regarding both of these cases was circulated to federally licensed gun dealers doing business in Kansas. The risk profile was significantly higher due to the higher standard of care required in Kansas.

You can leave your car keys on the bureau where your teenager can find them and drive off in your car—statistically more likely to lead to the injury and death of innocents than firearms—and that's not a problem in Kansas. Automobile sales companies must have more pull than federally licensed gun dealers.

Although dealers were warned about the situation, nothing was reported in the magazines of Kansas chiefs of police, sheriffs, and peace officers' associations. The Kansas attorney general was likewise silent. The Law Enforcement Training Commission apparently knew nothing of the decisions—either of which has a huge impact in terms of municipal liability where peace officers are issued guns belonging to the city, the county, or the state.

It's unlikely that Kansas will end up the only state applying strict liability to ownership and possession of firearms. It is quite likely that such pressure will be universal.

Regardless of the local rules, peace officers have to exert control over firearms, whether they are privately owned or agency owned, and personally possessed. The keys can't be where minors have access. That's too bad. There are cases on record where children have properly used firearms in defense of themselves and parents. That could happen in Kansas, although the sharp criminal offender would simply sue the victims and win a judgment.

Advanced Firearms Instruction Techniques

7

High Speed...

I was at a national training seminar and there was one lecture session I just had to take: Advanced Firearms Instructor Training. Representatives of the FBI, including Gary Hutchinson of the FBI Academy, were listed as presenters. The room was overfilled, literally standing room only. This was apparently a very popular class.

We were in Salon IV of the Marriott in Richmond, Virginia, and it was about 1:45 p.m. on January 14, 2000. The first PowerPoint slide came up on the screen. The title was "Understanding Marksmanship Fundamentals."

The seminar could be summed up in a sentence: "What do you misunderstand about the fundamentals?"

...Low Drag

I saw a post on an Internet shooting forum where a correspondent complained, "Everyone wants advanced range stuff." He went on to note that "advanced" means "mastery of fundamentals."

How do you define "mastery" in this context? You simply do it smoother, faster, and with more precision than the average bear. That's it.

For example, the main problem in shooting accuracy isn't sight alignment, sight picture, or stance. It's trigger jerking. Gary Hutchinson said that he was starting a program, Trigger Jerkers Anonymous, or TJA. We all jerk the trigger. Everyone who shoots does. The world-class champion shooter jerks the trigger. The most accomplished military sniper jerks the trigger. Jeff Cooper jerked the trigger. I do too, not because I want to—but because I can't always prevent it. We all jerk the trigger. What's the difference between a champion and a duffer?

It's all a matter of frequency and degree. Jeff Cooper jerked the trigger less often than I and to a lesser degree. New shooters do it more often and to a greater degree. Hutchinson said that 95% of all shooting errors were trigger control. We anticipate recoil and report. Part of precision shooting is the surprise break. Part of shooting in battle is the compressed surprise break. We want the shot to surprise. We do not want the shot to startle! To see the startle response as it relates to trigger control—or lack thereof—they use videos that can be slowed down to 1/30th a second. This is invisible to the naked eye, which can focus on the order of 24 times a second.

Showing us this high-speed video, we can see that the gun fires at 4/30th of a second. The gun is already low and sinking due to the shooter snatching at the trigger. It becomes a convulsive clutch at the trigger, dragging the muzzle off target at the moment of ignition.

We know how that happens. Jim Cirillo called it "framing the shot." The sights are aligned in our vision as they dance around the target. The shooter sees the gun moving about the target while trying to keep the front post centered and trimmed. When the sights move across the "x" ring, the shooter has the frame—everything is right for this moment, but the gun will soon move away. So the shooter slams on the trigger, moving the muzzle away from the mark.

It's simple to understand. It's just not easy to correct. In fact, Jeff Cooper said that trigger control is the hardest element to teach. We have to isolate the movement of the trigger finger from everything else. The trigger is ideally centered on the first pad of the finger. The distal joint is often seen as better to use when trigger length and weight of pull get longer—when using a revolver double-action trigger, for example. Ayoob calls the distal joint the "power crease" due to its superior leverage.

The location of the trigger finger isn't as critical as how that finger moves and what it drags against. Movement is from the second joint. Stretch a rubber band between the left thumb and the right index finger (for right-handed shooters). Move the rubber band back and forth simply by bending the index finger at the second joint. This is the independent motion drill. Try to keep lateral trigger finger pressure off the frame. My finger rubs against the Glock frame. It's thick enough it can't be helped, but it can be compensated for.

Advanced Trigger Control

Simply stated, there is one thing to learn about trigger control: Apply continuously increasing pressure to the trigger and allow the gun to fire. It's positive pressure. Do not start the trigger back, pause, restart, and pause again. Don't accelerate through the trigger press. If you hesitate, you will accelerate. When the muzzle is directed at the threat and you've formed the intention to fire, take the slack out of the trigger as the sights settle onto the target. Immediately begin application of constantly increasing pressure to the rear. Let the gun fire. Let the trigger forward to reset. Don't try to find the exact point of

Figure 7.1 This shooter holds the Browning Hipower with a high grip. The index finger is placed so the first pad is on the trigger. Notice that the thumb could touch the tip of the middle finger if the grip were closed a bit more—this is one indication of a properly sized handgun for this hand.

the reset, especially if you are rushed. At the same time, don't let your finger fly free of the trigger either. Keep a touch on it. Upon reset, apply constantly increasing pressure on the trigger if the target still stands. Repeat as needed. It's easily understood but devilishly difficult to accomplish consistently.

People tend to multitask while shooting. They're trying to move and draw while they identify the target. As the gun comes into line, they're trying to see sights, trying to ensure the grip (which should have been set while the gun was holstered), trying to roll the trigger back so the ignition will happen at just the right second. Then they're trying to "score the target" while they are resetting the trigger. The trainers at HK's International Training Division refer to the tendency to "score the target" while shooting as "eye sprints." The eye shifts focus from the sights to the target and back again.

They're moving the gun while they look over it. Usually the bullet's still in the bore while they're scoring. Similarly, when shooting at steel reactive targets, shooters tend to want to see the bullet hit the steel. Well, they can't. If they're looking at the steel, they miss the target. If they're looking at the sights, they can't see the bullet strike.

Figure 7.2 The same shooter as in Figure 7.1, with a Glock 19. It is slightly thicker and longer in grip from front to back, the thumb is almost too far back for proper fit. The index finger is a little short for a perfect fit to the trigger.

Figure 7.3 Jim Cirillo demonstrates trigger reset in front of a line of shooters.

Figure 7.4 Shooting on steel helps diagnose a student's tendency to focus on the target or to score the target while shooting ("eye sprints").

Grip is closely related to trigger control. In fact, the FBI Academy finds most of the problems to be trigger control followed by sight alignment–sight picture. In my experience, it's trigger followed by grip. Grip is often related to trigger control.

People often grip inconsistently. We find a lot of the new shooters will hold low on the backstrap. A certain percentage will go back to holding low on the backstrap without constant reminders. A smaller group will revisit low backstrap holds throughout their career. Since the passage of the Law Enforcement Officers Safety Act (LEOSA, H.R. 218), we've had retirees in for annual shooting tests, and I've seen the low backstrap hold by two of them.

Long shooting strings and long courses of fire mean grip fatigue and we'll see lapses in concentration as well. Some people just hold loosely. When they fire the gun, the whole hand will close and the rounds tend to be low, some completely below the target and target frame.

We can rehabilitate those shooters as well as those who can't seem to get the trigger control thing down by taping up the sights. Often having to read the sights while gripping the gun and manipulating a trigger is simply too much. Move them up to 3 or 5 yards, tack up an 8½ × 11 inch sheet of paper, and work on trigger and grip without sights. Simply taking the sights out of the equation can help in the short term. Conversely, a "negative" target can help. This is cutting a scoring circle out of the target, leaving one big hole

Figure 7.5 This trigger control exercise starts at one second per reset in the first circle, a half-second reset for the second circle, and full-tilt speed consistent with 100% hits in the circle. Note the brass shower out of this S&W 9mm.

centered on the silhouette. I want them to shoot through the hole, not touching paper or cardboard.

Gripping Suspense

A word about the grip is appropriate. Put the gun in hand so that the backstrap is centered in the "V" of the shooting hand, with the axis of the bore parallel with the forearm when the gun's fit to the shooter allows. The shooter's hand must be high on the backstrap. The non-gun or support hand can be high, with the heel of hand pressing inward against the frame and the non-gun wrist turned forward. The thumbs lay pointing forward without lots of pressure being exerted on the pistol.

The shooting hand's grip pressure is exerted front to rear, like pliers. Don't put a lot of side pressure on the gun. The shooting wrist is locked firmly with arms extended and locked, if possible. Some of us have enough joint and tendon issues that it won't work. Do not hyperextend the elbows. This will minimize the chances of tendon injuries. If you have a shooter with strength issues, have him or her hit the heavy bag. That will tighten the wrists up.

A bit of advice often given is, "Don't grip the gun too hard." I attended a class where we were told that no more than 40% of gripping power was to be in the shooting hand and no more than 60% in the support hand. How an

Figure 7.6 This shooter has the left wrist flexed, tilting the left hand forward and putting the pad of the palm against the open side of the pistol's grip frame.

Figure 7.7 While the elbows are close to being locked out—leading to joint injuries over time—this shooter's stance is more than enough for the gun (HK P2000 9mm).

Figure 7.8 This shooter has flexed elbows and has a pair in the air—shooting the powerful yet soft-shooting S&W M&P40.

officer can judge that in the midst of a gunfight went unexplained. That said, it's a technique that works well on the range when there are no judgment calls, no bystanders, and the shooter isn't injured.

Another trainer—one more into teaching how to fight than simply how to shoot—was asked how hard an officer should grip the handgun. "Hold onto it like your life depends on it," he replied.

The typical advice for a new learner is to grip the gun until it begins to shake with the tremors of overtensed muscles, then ease up a little. Others say that the ideal grip is like a firm handshake or like gripping a hammer when striking a nail.

I tend to the "harder is better" school of thought with some limitations. Basically, hold it as tightly as you can within reason. The grip needs to firm up the closer you are to a threat—it will tighten on its own when someone is trying to murder you. And the faster you shoot, the harder the grip needs to be.

Remember, we're trying to control service size or compact handguns with service loads against a deadly threat. Coarse accuracy quickly delivered is the order of the day unless you need to put on the brakes because the offender is using cover or you need to go for a round to the cranio-ocular cavity to stop the fight. This mission requires a strong grip.

Figure 7.9 The shooter has to be able to function from whatever position he or she ends up in. This shooter is working supine, careful of shooting past her extremities and with caution regarding the height of the impact berm.

Stance

This is a short section on stance. I've seen lots of descriptions, heard lots of discussions, and seen plenty of pictures to describe a shooting stance. If you're standing and, for one reason or another, can't move, get the gun out in front and shoot if that is indicated. There's no special need beyond that.

I've had people tell me that the shooter's feet should point in the direction he or she is firing. Or they should point slightly outboard, for balance. I've seen a presentation where we were told what percentage of weight goes on the rear leg and how much on the front leg. The problem we have is, what position will you be in when you have to shoot for real? We don't have that answer. The best response is to be able to shoot from whatever position you find yourself in.

Generally, your feet will be a little more than your shoulders' width apart. Your knees should be bent or at least flexed. Perhaps you should be ready to move, if you have warning something is about to happen.

Feet, knees, hips, and shoulders should be squared with whatever you need to shoot, if there is time to arrange it. Shoulders should be forward of the hips, which should be back. Don't stand straight up and don't have your shoulders level with the hips or behind them when standing straight and erect.

Figure 7.10 Our shooter works up from supine to sitting, fighting her way to her feet.

Figure 7.11 The shooter on the left has his muzzle level with the threat, with the empty case of the previous shot barely above the slide. The shooter on the right has a pistol in full recoil with the muzzle up. A better stance and firmer grip would have flattened that recoil curve considerably.

Figure 7.12 The aggressive stance will keep this muzzle level throughout the fight.

Look at the way a fighter stands during the fight. Emulate that. I've had a student disarm himself and grabbed his shirt as if grappling. He squared up to me, and lowered his center by bending his knees and throwing his hips back while moving his shoulders forward. "Good, that's how you stand to shoot."

It's a gunfight. Look like you're fighting.

Sights Are Good

Sights are good. As mentioned in an earlier example, someone went to a lot of time, trouble, and expense to put them on the gun. It seems a shame not to use them. By the same token, a national class trainer told a class I was in, "Inside of ten yards, the sights are overrated."

At the risk of controversy, I'm going to agree with that evaluation. The Gunsite School Drill is instructive in this regard. The first stage calls for a single shot to the triangle scoring area in the head box. This is taken from the holster to the hit in 1.5 seconds at 3 yards. I saw the sights, sort of. Even at that, I saw my sights much more clearly at 10, 15, and 25 yards. There wasn't a lot more time, but it was enough.

I just had a glimpse of them up close. What's the big deal? It wasn't what I *saw*, it was what I looked at. I needed a flat line across the top of the front

Figure 7.13 This is a classic sight picture: the front sight is in clear focus. While it's not perfectly centered in the rear notch and it's slightly over level with the top of the rear notch, good trigger control would make a decent hit at close range. At distance, we'd be high and right. The rear sight is properly blurred. Collect information around the top of the sights.

and rear sights to make the hit. Trigger control was vastly more important. I'd fired probably 8,000 rounds of ammunition through the same type of pistol I was using for that class. When you have that kind of experience with a sidearm, you'll be pointing in the right place.

The sights confirm the location of the muzzle relative to the target. Visual focus needs to be on the front sight. It is the sight closest to the muzzle and gives you the best reference on where the muzzle is pointing. Mental focus has to be on the information around the front sight. It's easier and faster to read that information when the visual focus is sharp on the front sight. For Jim Cirillo and Gary Hutchinson, they saw their sights when the shooting was for real. Others report they couldn't see their sights during the fight.

Since the human eye can focus on different distances quickly and the mind is operating on a different level during a fight, it's quite possible that the shooter's visual focus was on the front sight at the moment of ignition—and the shooter not able to recall that fact afterward. Battle (or incipient battle) is a potent elixir and it causes many changes in perceptions during and immediately after the fight.

Figure 7.14 This front sight is in focus. Being over the muzzle, it's the best indicator of the muzzle's location. Cirillo Visible Sights are shown.

Figure 7.15 The rear sight in focus. The front sight is blurred but still visibly centered. With these Cirillo Sights, a hit can still be made—the front sight is wonderfully prominent. The target is blurred past identification.

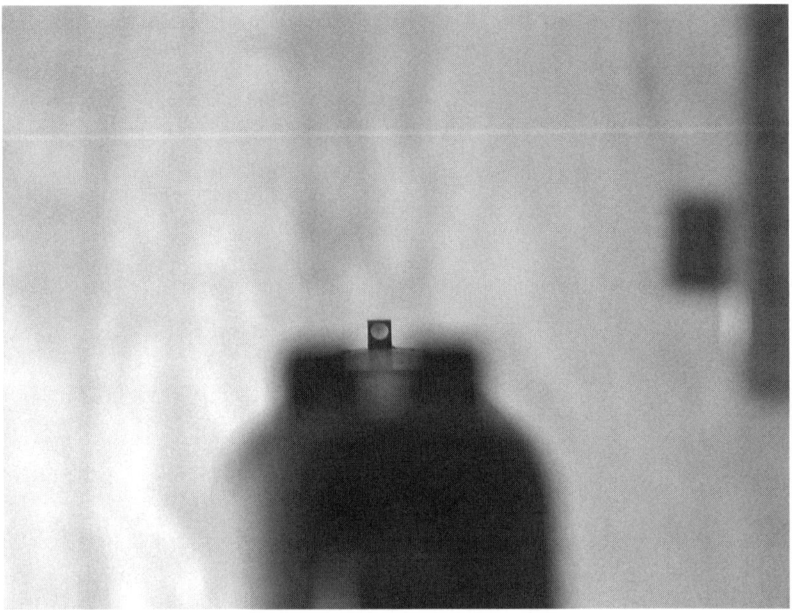

Figure 7.16 Here the front sight is in focus, but it's high over the rear notch. If held low on a threat in the manner of the StressFire Point Index, this would get a hit with proper trigger control.

Figure 7.17 The rear sight in focus. The front sight has wandered off, printing considerably right. Consider trying to line up on your killer with this view.

Figure 7.18 Jim Cirillo used a Ring's Training Gun fitted with Crimson Trace LaserGrips for classroom demonstrations of the natural arc of movement.

Shooters must do their best to get a perfect sight picture while realizing that getting that perfect sight picture is unlikely to the point of the impossible. Part of the reason is the arc of movement, or "wobble area."

The arc of movement is the normal movement of the pistol that occurs during aiming and firing. The best way to show new shooters is to have a laser on a model gun and a target posted in the class room. A molded training gun from Ring's Training Guns that is fitted with a Crimson Trace LaserGrip is ideal. This is the setup that was used by Jim Cirillo in his classes and one that I've co-opted.

I try to hold that laser dot still on the center of the target. The students watch the dot dance around inside the "five ring." Then I have individuals come up and try to hold it still. They quickly come to the conclusion that the gun is going to move around. Shooters have to accept this wobble area and shoot through the movement. They have to focus on applying constant and consistent pressure to the trigger, allowing the gun to fire inside that arc of movement.

Focus on the trigger first, sights second.

Aftermath

Allow the gun to fire. As it settles back on center from recoil, you've reset the trigger while still looking where the front sight was. This is follow-through. Just as important as when hitting a baseball or a golf ball or throwing a pass,

Figure 7.19 Jim had each student use the Ring's Training Gun with LaserGrips so he could assess their arcs of movement and to see how they see their sights.

follow-through is critical to shooting. It's compressed, like much in shooting. You're putting the hits where they are needed, then shifting to other targets or potential targets. To get those hits where you want them, you have to follow through. The gun can be moved, throwing a shot awry while the bullet's in the barrel.

Follow-through ends when the trigger is reset. Begin the next shot. The last shot in a planned string of shots is the one most likely to be thrown due to a lack of follow-through.

The Plan

Our priorities are simply stated. First, put constantly increasing pressure on the trigger, letting the gun fire. (Don't *make* it fire.) Accept and manage recoil. Concentrate on the data from the area of the front sight. Follow through.

Have your shooter shoot. Watch the shooter, not the target. Note errors or problems. Discuss those errors in the context of fundamentals. Test the pistol for sight adjustment. Test the student's sight alignment. Have the shooter shoot left-handed and right-handed.

You can test the student's sight alignment—the way he or she is looking at the sights—in a number of safe ways. One way is to use a molded Ring's Training Gun with Crimson Trace LaserGrips and to have the shooter aim at the target in the classroom. If you've cut the rear sight notch out on the training gun, there are sights to be used. Simply zero the laser to the iron sights at the distance the student will be aiming.

Figure 7.20 Use of a laser, like this LaserMax guide rod unit, are helpful in dry-fire and diagnosing problem shooters.

If your department guns have Crimson Trace units or LaserMax guide rod lasers, you can use them for the same thing as long as they're pointed in a safe direction. The lasers are also handy for dry-fire, where you watch the student's laser when he or she is dry-firing to see if there is a trigger control issue.

Another way is to have the student use his or her index finger for the front sight and the first two fingers of the other hand to use as the rear sight. Have the student aim at your eye using "finger sights." Look to see if the index finger is too high or low, or off to one side.

Peter Burlingame, a tactical firearms instructor since 1988, likes to remove the slide from the pistol and have the problem student use the *disembodied* slide to sight in on his eye. No student or instructor ever uses a gun to point at another human being, ever.

After checking the student's sight alignment, take the range and make ready. Have the student aim. The instructor does the trigger press for the student. First, the student keeps his or her index finger above the trigger guard on the frame; then the exemplar drill is accomplished with the instructor pressing through the student's index finger and the trigger. Do singles and pairs.

After that, we're left with practice. Dreary, drudging, and repetitive—it's required to make a decent shooter. If a student wants to be an advanced shooter, he has to practice, practice often, and practice as perfectly as possible.

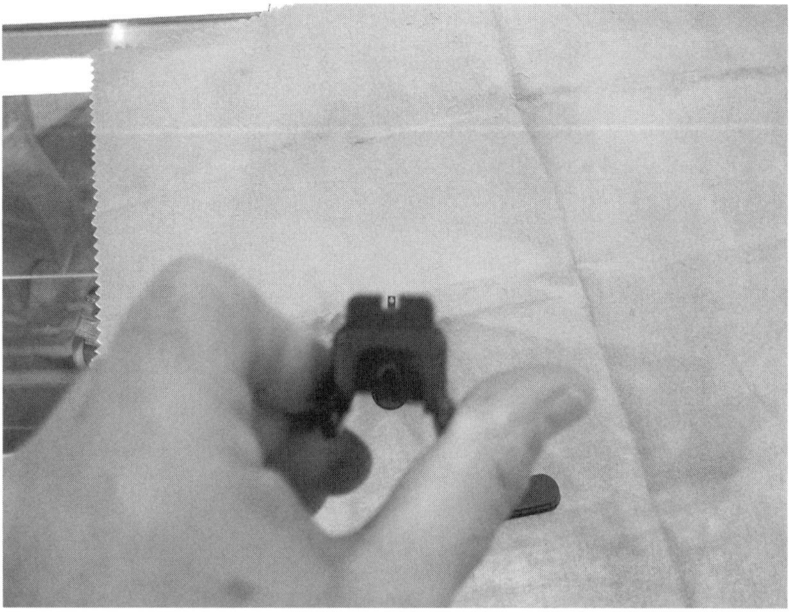

Figure 7.21 Taking the slide off the pistol and having the student point at your eye helps you determine what sight picture your student is seeing.

Advanced Firearms Instruction Seminar Session

It took only the first slide, the one that said "fundamentals of marksmanship," to make the room clear out. Advanced firearms means running and gunning, lots of targets, high speeds, and a few hits—at least, that's what it means to lots of people. Everyone wants to come to the party, but no one wants to stay and clean up.

We can't allow shooting to be mind-numbing drudgery for peace officers. If it is, they won't get good at it. If they're not good at it, there's a good chance they'll lose the fight and we'll have yet another police funeral.

That leaves it to instructors to make it fun, make it interesting, and make it relevant. We can ask, as Clive Shepherd always did, "Are you learning anything? Are we safe? Are you having fun?" He felt we couldn't be successful unless the students answered "yes" to all three questions.

Qualification Controversies and Courtroom Survival

8

I have appeared on a number of panels of "firearms training experts" at law enforcement seminars. I felt like a fraud, being on a panel with people like Bert DuVernay, Clive Shepherd, Massad Ayoob, Brian Felter, Vince O'Neill, Brian Stover, Bill Usilton, and Harvey Hedden.

I was impressed with the company I was keeping, but I was more impressed with the questions we received. The questions that had the most impact had to do with qualifications. Is it better to use pass-or-fail scoring or to actually keep a number? Which target is the best to use? Which course of fire? How often should our people qualify every year?

Qualifications? What was there to say? Most of the controversies I'd been aware of were dealt with years ago, or so I thought. Our audience, only some of whom were firearms instructors, had to have known that. Their questions made me reflect upon the changes in qualifications I'd seen over the years.

I can't seem to teach without learning. Their questions, and questions raised by our answers, included:

1. Should qualifications be pass-fail or scored?
2. What course should we use? How about shooting skills versus tactics?
3. Who can safely get out of night-fire or dim-light qualifications? We can leave day-shift officers and the office people out, right?
4. We don't have to shoot at 25 yards anymore, do we? Since most officers killed die within 10 feet of their attackers, why should we shoot at distance?
5. What targets should we be using?
6. How many times should we be qualifying? The more, the better, right?

I may not have definitive answers to all these questions, but the answers I have might lead us in the right direction.

The Pass-Fail Issue

Many years ago, my agency went to pass-fail qualification. At the time, we did this on the recommendation of the National Rifle Association, the folks who trained our firearms instructors.

I argued against the change. If we only count hits until the officer has passed and record simply a "pass," how does that look to a jury?

Remember what qualifications are: They are tests of skills and accuracy. I want to see if it's safe to allow you to roam about in public while you are armed. I operate on the presumption that, if you are in a shooting, I'll have to provide proof of your skills and accuracy in court.

Now, if I have a "P" by your name, what can I testify to? You passed.

"By how much?" plaintiff's counsel asks.

How do I know? All you had to do was pass.

"But did he barely pass? Did he nearly fail?"

I don't know.

"*You* don't know? You're the firearms instructor! Why don't you know?"

That's the way we do it.

"Okay," plaintiff's counsel says, sighing to alert the jury that he is exasperated. "Fine. Why do you not record qualification scores?"

Because, if we record scores, attorneys would ask more questions and increase our exposure to liability.

"You mean that, if you recorded scores, you would have to provide more information to the court?"

Yep.

Plaintiff's attorney smiles. "So, you did this to keep information from the court, right?"

Right again.

The judge won't be smiling. The jury will be wondering why we are trying to keep information from them. It looks like we have something to hide.

I wouldn't want to have to explain that in court.

I was overruled and we went to pass-fail scoring. It didn't last long. I spoke to another member of a panel I was on, someone who was at the time a representative of the NRA Law Enforcement Activities Division, and I remarked that the NRA had jumped on the pass-fail bandwagon without a lot of thought. "We've since fixed that," he said.

NRA still gives "passes" and "fails" when the scores go in to headquarters, but they maintain a record of scores and other pertinent information about the qualification test.

There are other good reasons to keep score. For example, pass-fail rewards poor shooters and punishes good shooters. If you're a consistent 95% shooter and we go to a pass-fail system, now you're just another "pass." The guy who shot a score of just 71% passed as well as you did. Our aim is not to reward poor shooters while hurting the dedicated shooter.

It has also been pointed out that pass-fail scoring denies the diagnostic function of qualification. If you have a consistent 70% to 74% shooter, you have an obvious problem. This officer is attaining the primary standard (not "minimum standards"), but he isn't improving. If your only record is "pass," you can't even see that a problem exists.

Our younger officers like to use qualification scores to compete against each other. This adds a pressure to qualification that doesn't exist otherwise. The competition pressure shows the student his or her weaknesses and gives him or her a way to work on those weaknesses.

The Question of Tactics

Wouldn't it be a better test of firearms skill to include tactics? Sure. In fact, a number of our experts called for options like reactive targets, movement to cover, and multiple targets.

Remember what we're discussing: qualification. Qualification can be defined as "a documented standard of achievement." How are tactics to be scored? There are ways, but the problem is that scoring tactics is subjective. How can we do so fairly and accurately?

Some movement is reportedly incorporated by certain agencies. I'd heard that the Arizona Department of Public Safety had incorporated movement into the course of fire, such that each officer on a line has to take a side step as the targets turn. That's not tactical qualification, but it's a start.

I suggest you put qualification and tactics in separate categories. Qualification amounts to an exam. Records of qualification are discoverable evidence in civil and criminal trials. Marking someone off for "failure to use cover" could be seen as an actionable lack of competence. If your people do anything beyond marksmanship, that's tactics and has to do with training, not qualification.

The best blend is to put items of cover out for each officer. When the targets turn, each shooter has to safely draw as he or she steps behind cover. It wouldn't hurt to put photocopied images of guns on each target. That way, no officer would fire without moving to cover and no officer would ever fire at a target that wasn't showing a threat. To further create realism, have the officers challenge the targets verbally.

Why Day-Shift Officers Need Dim-Light Shooting

Many years ago a California officer, working a day watch, entered a house to check the welfare of a resident who hadn't recently been seen. There was no response when the officer knocked on the door. The officer, in the dark house without a flashlight, had been taught by his instructors that no one ever used a flashlight in real nighttime shootouts. He'd never trained to use a flashlight and didn't think he needed one.

His worst nightmare began when he saw the moving human silhouette with a gun in hand. He performed the appropriate response to a sudden gun threat. Unfortunately, the silhouette was a small child, who was "armed" with a toy gun. The media and the local and state government subsequently called for bans on toy guns. They didn't call for dim-light training or dim-light qualification.

More officers than ever before are carrying flashlights all the time, even during the day. It's possible that the officer will work off-duty security at night. It's equally possible that the officer will work some hours of darkness, such as those very early in the morning. And there's always the chance that "it" will come to you when you're off duty.

Train in dim light. It probably wouldn't hurt to fire a qualifying course in dim light, to prove to yourself and the trainers that you can do it. If you can do it in dim light, you can make it in daylight. I tried to ensure that everyone had to shoot in conditions of adverse light during an agency-wide transition to another auto pistol. It was a familiarization course, but it gave everyone an idea of how the new guns differed from the old.

Why We Still Shoot at Distance

Most officers killed by felonious action are killed at a distance from 0–10 feet. Look at those figures; that's not yards, it's feet. I raise this issue of distance in the Weapon Retention classes I teach. I ask what this figure means, hoping students will cite the lack of a reactionary gap.

I had one student who said, "It proves we're wasting our time shooting at 25 yards." I couldn't suppress a heavy sigh.

His answer wasn't even in the neighborhood. It proves that action beats reaction. It proves that we *don't die* in fights where we have distance on our side. It proves that our ability to take cover and use time to our advantage leads to victory.

Why can't we shoot at 25 yards? When I started in police work, many departments were still qualifying with courses that included shooting at the 50-yard line. Now the crying is loud and long when the 25-yard line is used. "I won't shoot at anyone who's 25 yards away," some say. "I'll just hide or maybe I'll retreat."

If the offender is armed with a rifle, even a .22 rifle, that kind of technique won't lead to victory. It will lead to crippling injury or death, possibly yours. Or it could lead to the death of a citizen you had a duty to protect.

Some believe that a qualification course that includes 25-yard shooting certifies you to shoot at 25 yards and closer. Four of us on one panel mentioned an ability to shoot at 25 yards as a primary standard. Another said his agency still has a 50-yard line for handgun qualifications.

Figure 8.1 Dim-light shooting is required for day-shift personnel. Some buildings don't have power, or the day-shift people may be forced to work at night or to engage threats off duty. The officer over the top has a gun-mounted light. The other officer is using a handheld light. Lights courtesy of Surefire.

The fact is, we don't get to pick the distance over which our lethal "marksmanship exercise" will occur. The offender gets to choose. Don't shortchange yourself or your students; fire some percentage of your qualifications at 25 yards. It could save a life.

Figure 8.2 In an instructor class, groups were formed to plan qualification courses. Each group had a different target to use and had different constraints—maximum distance on the range, state requirements, and so on.

What else should the course include? Since it's a test of competencies, determine what skills are necessary on the street. List these and find a way to train to these skills. After training, test these skills regularly.

It's important that an officer be able to holster safely. It's a vital skill for officers who carry traditional double-action pistols. I've seen a number of folks on the calmest firing range try to holster a weapon while it's still cocked! Obviously, fingers should be free of the trigger guard.

It's important to be able to safely draw, particularly if the holster used has a complicated retention system. I can remember my time at the state academy as a basic trainee, but I can't remember any training in drawing a sidearm from a holster. Perhaps they expected us to get the technique from television.

In any event, have your officers draw from a snapped holster. It may come as some surprise to note that many officers leave the magazine pouches and holsters unsnapped so they can beat the stopwatch. This doesn't help on the street, as the smart cop keeps duty gear secured at all times. We don't want them to tug helplessly at their secured pistol while an amused attacker looks on.

Obviously, officers need to be able to load, do quick reloads, and unload their firearms. It's easy to take these basics for granted, but it's silly to do so. Make them demonstrate their competency. Make them incur stoppages and clear them.

Figure 8.3 Traditional double-action (DA) autos are cocked after firing. They must be "decocked" before holstering.

Figure 8.4 The decocking lever is used to make the traditional DA auto safe for holstering. This has to be watched during training and qualification.

Figure 8.5 Use of the decocker is something to test in the standards—a documentable standard of achievement beyond the qualification.

Figure 8.6 Students must be able to safely holster sidearms. This shooter has the trigger finger up on the frame away from the trigger and his thumb behind the slide—preventing him from pushing the slide out of battery during reholstering. His non-gun hand is on his chest, out of the way. Unfamiliar with this rig, this shooter is wisely watching the process.

Figure 8.7 With the gun holstered, he uses one hand to refasten the thumb break snap. This is an all-too-rare skill.

Qualification does not take the place of training. Train them, then test their proficiency via a qualification course.

The Best Course

The best course to use to qualify your troops is the course your state mandates. If you're in a state where there is no mandated course, use the NRA's Instructor Development Qualification Course. NRA Law Enforcement Activities Division would be happy to send a list of courses they've developed over the years.

If, for some reason or another, you are prevented from using anything from the NRA, check into getting a copy of the International Association of Law Enforcement Firearms Instructors' Range Standards book. You might consider joining IALEFI if you're the department's firearms instructor, so you can network with other instructors. I've found the International Law Enforcement Educators and Trainers Association (ILEETA) to be particularly helpful in that regard too.

What targets do we use? It depends on the course of fire. In fact, when Clive Shepherd was with the NRA, he said that he liked to have agencies make calls on each other, packing about a hundred targets along. "Ask to trade a hundred of yours for a hundred of theirs. Then, have your troops

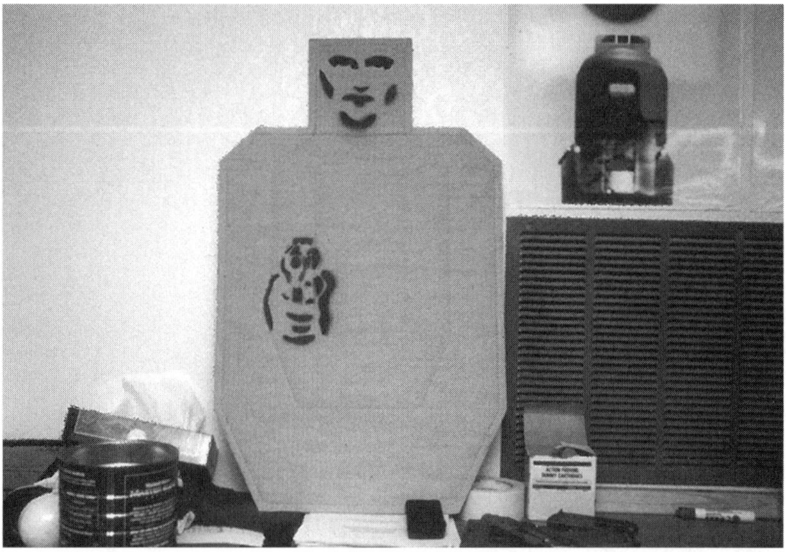

Figure 8.8 This target has a face and a threat (gun)—both painted on. It is appropriate for training and for qualification.

shoot on different targets periodically." A few panel members used sheets from a legal pad. I checked our department's old target, the NRA TQ-15. The highest scoring zone is slightly wider and a little shorter than an 8½ × 11 sheet of paper.

Other agencies have gone to International Practical Shooting Confederation (IPSC) targets due to the more challenging scoring zones.

The bottom line: If a particular course calls for a particular target, use that target. If it's not available, use what you can get. Vary the courses and vary the targets. That gives the best picture of a trainee's skill level (Figure 8.12).

Some institutions combine a qualification course of fire with the standards drill. The standards are a cluster of skills that each student has to individually demonstrate for an instructor. Instead of having a line of shooters and not knowing precisely what each individual is doing, the instructor has one trainee on the line and watches his or her every move. A relevant skill might be "Load." If there is a particular protocol for loading a sidearm, the student demonstrates that procedure for the instructor's approval. If there is a problem, it is remediated on the spot. If, after three attempts, the trainee demonstrates that he or she doesn't know "the Deal," it's time for some retraining.

My first exposure to the standards as explained here was at the HK International Training Division during their Tactical Pistol Course. My state's law

Figure 8.9 Use of painted faces and threat indicators can also be used in decision-making exercises. Note the target in the middle has his hands up.

enforcement training academy has instituted a standards proficiency test in basic academy. While it has differences from the HK standards, they cover the items they feel are the most needed for academy recruits.

Figure 8.10 Use of photocopied face and threat indicators as well as a sheet of paper for hits to the pelvic region personalize the targets, making them better for training and qualification.

Figure 8.11 Your students need to work out on various targets and not just stick to one target or course of fire.

I made an accuracy test and a standards drill for our transition to new guns. There was no statewide qualification course at the time. I had each shooter put 10 hits on a standard sheet of typing paper from 15 yards. Each sheet was signed and maintained as a record of achievement. They trained back to 25 yards and up to contact distance. They executed the standards, one student at a time, while others watched. The standards included drawing and safe reholstering, stoppage clearances, gunpoint drills, pivots and turns, and unload, show clear. See Table 8.1 through 8.5 for copies of these standards.

The standards reflected parts of the course we determined were the critical parts of the training. There was shooting as part of the standard drills and the accuracy standard had to be maintained with no misses allowed. The standards are scored pass-fail with notes for each performance.

Regarding frequency of qualification, I let the state guide my decision. If the state requires all officers to successfully complete the state's course of fire once per year, I would ensure they did so. Firing more than one state course per year wastes training time and ammunition.

Use that time and ammo to train. Incorporate movement, cover, and discretionary decision making, among other things. Firing a qualification

Figure 8.12 Qualification courses are usually line drills—a number of shooters are on the line at one time. This prevents one-on-one examination—the instructor can't see everything everyone is doing.

Figure 8.13 Clearing stoppages and doing reloads are best tested in standards drills but can be used in qualifications as well.

Figure 8.14 You can include cover drills in qualification, forcing shooting from various positions.

course more than once doesn't make one "more qualified." What are you "qualified" to do anyway? When you pass once in a year, call it good. If you had a particularly tough time making hits at 25 yards, practice that phase. Slow to reload? Work on that skill. Don't shoot the whole course. Doing so

Figure 8.15 Shooting with the non-gun hand is a valuable thing to learn.

Figure 8.16 One-handed shooting is very likely in gunfights, often by necessity. This has to be experienced and should be tested.

repetitively simply ensures you can memorize the course of fire. It does nothing else to make you safer on the street, the range, or in the courthouse.

Remember, qualification is a test of accuracy and skills. Test the skills your people are likely to need "out there." If they're deficient, work with them. Make them better. Make sure they go home, in one piece, at the end of their shifts.

Figure 8.17 Standards drills are tested individually. Note the instructor on the left with an electronic timer as the shooter performs.

Figure 8.18 If you allow them to carry guns in ankle holsters, they need to draw from them.

Figure 8.19 Qualification is a test of skill, but the only remnant of that test is the score on the target.

Figure 8.20 Shooting "geared up" in uniform, wearing armor and duty equipment, makes sense.

Table 8.1 Tactical Revolver Course (TRC)

Distance	Shots Fired, Time Limits, and Positions
7 yards	12 shots in 25 seconds
15 yards	12 shots in 30 seconds
15 yards	6 shots with gun in strong hand, 6 shots in weak hand, all in 35 seconds, including reload
25 yards	6 shots kneeling, 6 shots left-handed in a standing barricade position, and 6 shots fired with right hand in a standing barricade position, all in 90 seconds—including reloads
25 yards	6 shots in a standing position, without artificial support, in 12 seconds

This is a 60-shot course, with each shot worth a maximum of 5 points, for 300 points possible. If this course is too easy, shoot each stage in half the time.

Table 8.2 NRA Distinguished Expert Qualification Course*

Stage	Distance	Position	No. of Rounds	Stage Time
1	25 yards	Kneeling, barricade	6 shots, strong side	
		barricade for cover	12 fired, shooter's choice	75 sec.
2	15 yards	Standing for:	6 shots, then	
		Kneeling for:	6 (Cover may be used if available)	25 sec.
	15 yards	Standing	6 shots	12 sec.
3	7 yards	Standing	12 shots	20 sec.
4	3 yards	Standing, strong hand	6 (1 hand only)	
		Standing, weak hand	6 (1 hand only)	
		(Starting from Ready Gun position)		20 sec.

* 60 rounds fired with a service handgun.
Times include reloads. Revised January 1986.

Table 8.3 Glock Transition Course (2003)

	Weapons Handling Standards Drills
1.	Drills will be conducted from the 6-yard line, utilizing the TQ-15 target (or the KLETC-Q, or the FBI/IALEFI-Q using the bottle as scoring areas).
2.	On the KLETC-Q and TQ-15, only hits inside the four and five rings will count as scoring hits.
3.	Student will repeat the drill until required hits are achieved. A miss stops the procedure.
4.	Student will start with all magazines loaded with three rounds. Instructor will have to add or subtract rounds in magazines for the particular drill.
1st Drill Load	Student will use the proper technique to load the weapon. Pass-fail.
2nd Drill in Battery Reload	Student will start with the weapon secured in the holster. The student will be instructed to fire two rounds on the signal, do an in-battery reload, and fire another two rounds. Must have four hits in the scoring area.
3rd Drill Out of Battery Reload	Student will start with the weapon secured in the holster. Student will start with two rounds in the weapon and two rounds in the next magazine to be loaded into the weapon. The student will be instructed to fire two rounds on the signal, do an out of battery reload, and fire another two rounds. Must have four hits in scoring area.
4th Drill Fail to Fire Malfunction	Student will start with the (chamber empty) weapon secured in the holster. Student will place a magazine with two rounds into the weapon while secured in the holster. The student will be instructed to fire two rounds on command. Students must pull the trigger after the muzzle is on target and before clearing the malfunction. Must have two hits in the scoring area.
5th Drill Fail to Eject Malfunction (Stovepipe)	Student will set up the stove pipe, and then insert a magazine with two rounds. Student will start from the firing position. The student will be instructed to properly clear the malfunction and fire two rounds on command. Must have two hits in the scoring area.
6th Drill Pivots and Turns	The student will demonstrate pivots and turns as follows: Each time, students will start in *Holstered.* The student will face to the right (left side toward the target) and, on signal, turn to face the target while in the act of drawing the pistol. The student will put two hits in the scoring area. The same procedure will be used for facing left (right side to the target) and facing uprange. Six hits will be required in the scoring area of their target. [Note to readers: The safety circle is taught in the class and is used in the standards.]
7th Drill Cover Drill	Each student will draw to *Guard*, demonstrating a gunpoint position (muzzle depressed, finger off trigger). On each call, the student will place one hit center mass to stop the threat. Repeat six times for six hits in the scoring area.

Table 8.3 Glock Transition Course (2003) (Continued)

	Weapons Handling Standards Drills
8th Drill Unload and Show Clear	Student will start with weapon secured in holster and a round in the chamber. On command student will properly administratively unload and clear weapon. Pass-fail.

24 hits total are required to pass.
9/23/2003
Added in 2004: Phase II clearance (rip, tuck, rack, reload) and movement with the gun.
Added in 2005: Shooting on the move—box drill—was added.

Table 8.4 Precision Shooting Standard Drill

Place an 8½ × 11 sheet of paper in the center of a clean backer. Students will fire 10 *consecutive* hits from 15 yards into the page. Nicks don't count. There is no time limit and the shooter can use his or her preferred stance. No one can approach the page or back away from it. Shooters can rest between rounds. (This is a standard of achievement in addition to the Basic Standards Drills.) (10 hits)

Table 8.5 Gunsite School Drills

250
3 yards, single head, 1.5 seconds, 2 times, 10 points
5 yards, 2 rounds to the body, 1.5 seconds, 10 points
7 yards, 2 rounds to the body, 1.5 seconds, 10 points
10 yards, 2 rounds to the body, 2 seconds, 10 points
15 yards, 2 rounds to the body, standing to kneeling, 3.5 seconds, 10 points
25 yards, 2 rounds to body, standing to prone, 7 seconds
El Presidente: par time 10 seconds, 60 points possible
For every second over 10, subtract 5 points from numerical score.
350
3 yards, single head, 1.5 seconds, with movement, 2 times, 10 points
7 yards, 2 rounds to the body, 1.5 seconds, with movement, 10 points
10 yards, 2 rounds to the body, 2 seconds with movement, 10 points
25 yards, 2 rounds to the body, standing to kneeling, 3.5 seconds with movement, 10 points
35 yards, 2 rounds to the body, standing to prone, 7 seconds with movement (step forward), 10 points
499
All shots are to the body
Two targets:
3 yards, 2 rounds per target, 2 seconds, 20 points
7 yards, 2 rounds per target, 3 seconds, 20 points
10 yards, 2 rounds per target, 5 seconds, 20 points
25 yards, 2 rounds per target, 6 seconds, 20 points
Single target:
35 yards, 2 rounds, standing to kneeling, 4 seconds, 10 points
50 yards, 2 rounds, standing to prone, 8 seconds, 10 points

9 Consolidating Force Training: Defensive Tactics and Firearms Instruction

Real World

A police officer makes contact with an apparently intoxicated subject at the site of a disturbance. The person is noncompliant. Silly at first, he becomes irritated and belligerent as the officer attempts to gain control. Starting with passive resistance, he moves to actively resist by pulling away and putting distance between himself and the officer. When the officer closes with him, the suspect swings a fist. Now actively resisting while using assaultive means, the officer's response options multiply.

As our offender simply fails to comply with lawful instructions, the officer can use verbal controls and may guide the offender with open hands. As he becomes actively resistive, the officer can grab and grasp. He can draw and display a club and—if he has received instruction in grappling using a club—can use it to reinforce armlock control measures. The officer isn't striking our flummoxed hero but is closing, grasping, and grabbing while still able to issue verbal instructions and lesser force options. As the drunk makes a fist and swings at the officer, the officer can respond with blocks and strikes to nonlethal and noncrippling targets on the offender's body. He can, of course, use techniques below that level of resistance if those options become available and have a reasonable chance of working.

Stymied by the officer's skills and persistence, our drunken suspect—still not in control of his reasoning mechanism—pulls a knife. The officer sees it.

Reasonable Responses

Now what? Well, an instructor of aerosol subject restraints (currently some form of oleoresin capsicum [OC]) might advise the officer to spray a pattern while moving out of the line of attack. An instructor of the club might teach blocks, strikes, and quick movement out of the kill zone. After all, the offender "just has a knife."

After looking at autopsy photos of people victimized by offenders who were armed "only with a knife," the firearms instructor might be talking

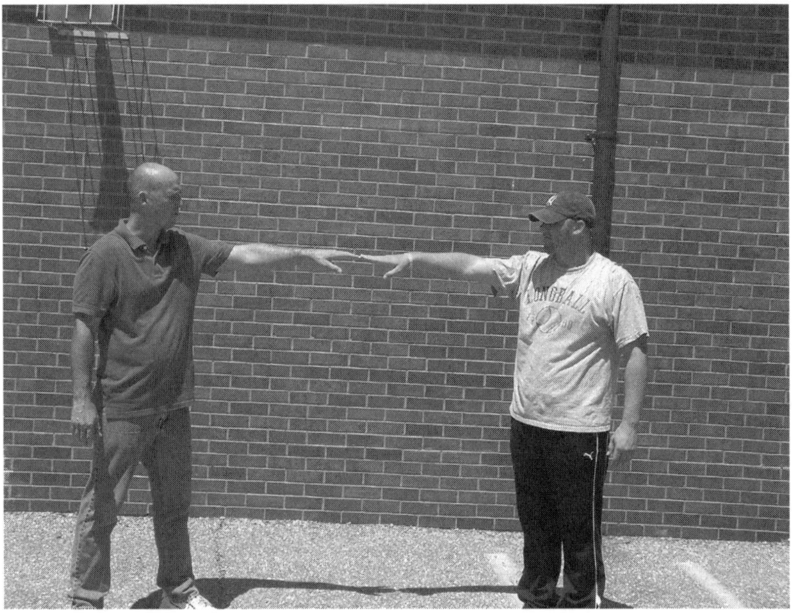

Figure 9.1 Learning to judge distance isn't easy. This simple demonstration shows a "normal" reactionary gap.

about extreme close-quarters deadly force application. (Put aside for the moment that three commercial airliners full of passengers and crew were taken over by a small minority of passengers armed "only with box cutters" on September 11, 2001—the death toll from the use of those edged weapons went over 3,000 people.)

What is the reasonable response? Where you end up depends on where you started. Because we have subject matter experts, not "force instructors," we have a situation that spells legal and moral disaster.

There was an organization called the American Society of Law Enforcement Trainers (ASLET) that used to hold annual training conferences around the United States during the first part of every year. I was invited to teach at one of these conferences at the Grapevine/DFW Airport, Texas, in January 1996. The theme of the conference was "Teaching Force across the Continuum," or some such thing. I got to sit in on various classes and found a pervasive thread that we consolidate all force topics into one Use of Force Instructor (UFI) course.

We had firearms instructors, defensive tactics (DT) instructors, defensive aerosols instructors, baton instructors, and the list went on. For a particular force problem, we have to go to the specialist for that level of force. When an officer is confronted with resistance, he or she has to determine the proper force level and use that force properly. We expect more of the students than the teachers.

Figure 9.2 This firearms/defensive tactics instructor shows how he talks to combative individuals. His hands are above his waist, almost giving the appearance of appeasement or supplication.

The solution most commonly accepted was to consolidate force options into a single instructor. The firearms instructor was the DT instructor, the baton instructor, the OC instructor, and the tactical communication officer.

As this is written, that ASLET seminar came and went nearly 12 years ago. What has changed since then?

Figure 9.3 The officer (left) is trying to appease a combative subject. Note the finger-pointing—psychological "cornering."

Figure 9.4 The offender (right) has closed the distance and grabbed the officer—who returns the favor. Note the officer's stance—feet about shoulders' width apart, left foot forward, with shoulders ahead of his hips and "nose over the toes."

Figure 9.5 "Let go!" The officer (left) "changes the channel" by giving his opponent something to consider. This is a precursor to control and custody.

UFI

Some years back, I was speaking to a member of a high-level law enforcement training academy. This was a place that is known as a benchmark standard of the law enforcement training community. When I was discussing consolidation, I was told, "Soft pedal that. The defensive tactics guys jealously guard their bailiwick and the firearms instructors are no better. They're afraid they'll lose some of their time, funding, or special status if they give anything up."

I subsequently sponsored a 2-week course taught by a mentor and colleague. Called DTI, or Defensive Tactics Instructor, the class covered elements of the Monadnock Defensive Tactics System, Gary Klugewicz's Active Countermeasures, Jim Lindell's Handgun/Long Gun Retention and Disarming System, a handcuffing and restraints system, tactical verbal communications, and the Monadnock Expandable Baton Instructor courses. Due to time constraints, we didn't do aerosol restraint, firearms, or PR-24 baton. DTI gave a pretty good spread, but it was just a start.

A consolidated use of force instructor would have a pretty daunting training resume. It's not easy to be the jack of all trades, but we expect our police professionals to be just that. They have to be able to (1) make the "most right" force decision, (2) in circumstances that are tense, uncertain, and

Figure 9.6 Gun teachers have to be force teachers. This instructor is demonstrating disarming techniques.

rapidly evolving, and (3) effectively, appropriately execute the use of force and use any force tools properly. This doesn't happen in a gymnasium or on a range. It happens on the street, in a home, a hospital, a school, or a shopping center. There are other people around, some involved in the situation. Others are bystanders.

Figure 9.7 In the DTI (Defensive Tactics Instructor) class, students learned how to teach empty-hand techniques, batons, and handcuffing among other things.

The events leading up to the resistance will be painstakingly examined to determine if the officer "predictably precipitated a need to use force." Everything said before, during, and after the force transaction will be examined. In fact, they'll likely try to look into the officer's background to find a predilection to use force—this using the wonderfully clear vision only capable in 20/20 hindsight.

When the use of force is examined and the officer is dissected, inevitably they'll come to look at the officer's training. As force transactions often, though not always, begin with a low-level force transaction before it escalates to homicide or grievous injury, they'll be looking at the instructors of those lesser force techniques and tools. The answers they get from those trainers will be matched to what they got from the firearms instructors.

When there is a disparity, liability lawyers have a way to winnow in. Even if it weren't for the lawyers, the officers who take classes in varying force levels from people with different training and perspectives can see the difference. The confusion placed thus can cause a lag in decision making and can cost lives. Let's get together.

Force

If you are a firearms instructor now, you can get pigeonholed into categories. "This is our rifle instructor," I'll hear when being introduced to a group. The others, I'll ask? "They're firearms instructors," will be the response.

A rifle *is* a firearm. If the rifle barrel is short and the piece weighs in at 6–9 pounds stripped (no flashlights, vertical grips, etc.), it's a carbine. Do you have a carbine instructor and a rifle instructor?

I hope not. A firearms instructor should be capable in as many types of firearms as an officer is likely to use or encounter. That said, the firearms instructor also needs to be a handcuffing instructor. Offenders who are gunshot get handcuffed, don't they?

A firearms instructor should be able to teach effective verbal control tactics. Do we not verbalize prior to and immediately after a shooting incident? Likewise, the fight might have started out with open hands, gone to aerosols or electronic discharge weapons (e.g., Taser), and then to the baton. Shouldn't our firearms instructors be able to learn these well enough to teach their use?

I've been on the stand testifying about use of force. An officer was on trial, and one of the questions I got had to do with whether I was a qualified OC instructor. I wasn't and OC hadn't been used in that incident anyway, but the question had been used to minimize the impact of my testimony in the eyes of the jury.

Figure 9.8 At a firearms instructor seminar (IALEFI Regional Training Conference [RTC]), an OC defense class was taught. The instructor—certified in guns and OC spray instruction—taught the gun guys how to teach a response to OC.

Figure 9.9 The best way to deal with spray is avoidance followed by disarming.

Figure 9.10 Each participant had to be exposed to an OC assault, had to use verbalization skills, move to a firing point, and knock down steel targets. The OC class was, surprisingly, a hit of the show.

Any instructor who teaches any force tool or technique must be able to skillfully articulate the standards for the use of force. I cringe when I hear someone pontificate about "rules of engagement." Appropriate on the battlefield when facing foreign military combatants, such concepts are irrelevant in American law enforcement.

I insist that our firearms instructors know the Fourth Amendment standard explained in *Graham v. Conner* as well as the "gun case" that was *Tennessee v. Garner*. Similarly, baton instructors and empty-hand tactics instructors have to know the gun cases as well. They also need to know gun tactics.

Across the Range

An eminent group of force trainers said it before the turn of the current century: We need to consolidate force instructors across the range of force options available to our officers. We need to be able to teach in one voice, to take an officer trainee from verbalization through lower levels of force, up to deadly force, and then back down again. We need to be conversant in de-escalation techniques. If the officer is a smooth talker, the need for force is minimized.

The best fight in the world is the fight we don't have. Everyone wins when there is no physical confrontation. If it takes force, use force that is objectively reasonable and stop using force when the offender stops resisting. Do appropriate custody and control and execute a high-risk search. Check into the offender's condition: "Are you injured?" even if he is cursing and calling you names.

If you are currently a firearms instructor, get thee to a physical custody–defensive tactics instructor course forthwith. Once that's complete, move on to batons and handcuffs. Strive to be a rounded instructor.

Any firearms instructor—and instructors in any force option or tool—must also be gun retention instructors. More on that appears in Chapter 10.

Gun Retention and Disarming

10

Proxemics

Firearms and defensive tactics go together like oil and water. Gun teachers tell us that distance is our friend, and DT-types tell us we have to "invade the offender's center" by getting way closer than we want. The firearms community has, in the past, given us a straight-up stance that is locked and rigid. The grappling community likes to "lower our center."

There was no way I would buy into the consolidation of force instruction if I hadn't had to do it myself. The bridge between range world and mat world was training to teach gun retention and disarming. Along with that came the realization that so many of our people die at ranges best measured in inches or a very few feet rather than the longer-than-realistic 7 yards of "close combat."

Close combat is being on the ground with a criminal on top of you while he sticks you with a knife. Any time I see firearms instruction programs that purport to teach "extreme close-quarters fighting," I make a mental bet with myself to see how long it takes for them to get people shooting at 5, 7, and 10 yards away. It's usually pretty quick.

The reality is that officers get killed up close because they don't know that there is going to be a fight. They think they're there to interview this guy, get his driver's license, ask a few questions, maybe write a citation, and then cut him loose.

The subject knows that his dead mother-in-law is in the trunk of the car, that he's been convicted already on two of his "three strikes and you're out." Not looking forward to a long stretch and seeing a complacent cop get too close, he does the math.

The offender knows his past. He knows whether or not he'll fight and often knows how much he's willing to do to get away. He knows when the fight will start and what weapons he has to use. Unlike us, he doesn't need a crystal ball. He doesn't need to learn to read body language or to listen and interpret what's being said "between the lines." All he has to do is wait until you look down at his license or until you're distracted by traffic or someone else. He knows what he'll do and he knows when and how.

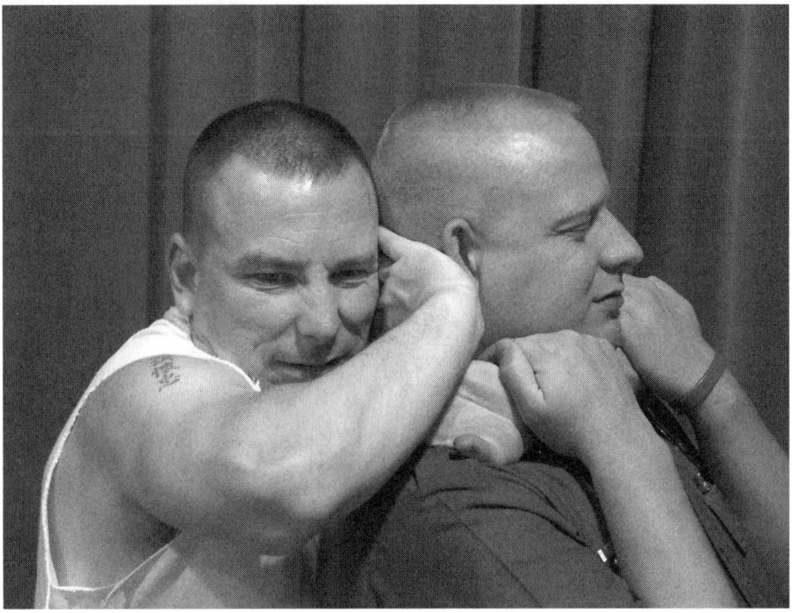

Figure 10.1 The offender knows if he's going to fight, when it's going to happen, and how far he's willing to go—as this uniformed officer found out.

We end up with a dead or crippled officer. An investigation is launched criminally to go along with the investigation to see what went wrong. If we've trained, it's too little. Or we spent time shooting from 25 yards or using the sights or any one of a number of other excuses.

The problem is we get too close before we're ready. We're not wary. We failed to read and understand the chapter of this book—or a number of other books—on mind-set.

So, before we go strolling up to chat with someone, we'll play a game called "What if?" What if he grabs my holstered handgun? What if he pulls a knife? Which hand is he likely to use? His dominant hand is the one he will likely open with, but which hand is that? Have you looked?

The rule of officer survival in any encounter is to have a plan. Look for problems, assume the worst, and prepare. Know from where the attack may come and have a counter in place at all times.

Consistent Stance

Making the transition from firearms instruction to hands-on defense and control was made easier by use of the consistent stance. Apparently, firearms instructors figured out that most firearms trainees aren't gun people. They don't

Figure 10.2 Extreme stances put all the power in one direction and inhibit quick movement off the line of attack.

specialize. Besides, it's harder to hit a target in motion than a stationary target. It's also harder to shoot accurately while in motion. Therein lies the solution.

The most likely stance found in gunfighting is where you end up when the bullets are flying. One tendency is to lower your center by flexing the knees and bending forward from the waist. When a missile goes flying by, we tend to lower ourselves. An examination of role-play training, simulations, or reality-based training shows that people get way low when the pellets are flying. Viewing patrol car and surveillance videos of shootings show the same stance by the participants. They didn't train in the same place, so there must be another reason why they go low.

In the mat room, square off with another officer. Have a trainer there, for safety and control. When the tussle begins, the trainer will order "Freeze!" Look at the stance you are both in. When you are struggling with someone else, you seek to keep your balance. The lowered, shoulders-forward stance enhances balance and allows quick movement.

On the range, take that stance with the handgun. Remember, stance isn't the way the arms are out, bent, or straight. It's not Weaver and it's not isosceles. Stance is the way the trunk, legs, and feet are arranged. The arms ahead of the shoulders are quite independent.

Figure 10.3 The shooter on the left is more aggressive in stance, though either could move and shoot from his platform.

Figure 10.4 When fast shooting is called for, move in on the gun.

Figure 10.5 This stance is more severe, but the user is controlling the 12-gauge shotgun with express loads.

Once that stance is identified with the handgun, try it with the shotgun. Bring the buttstock in toward the center of the body, allowing the toe of the stock to press into the shoulder pocket. The heel of the butt will likely extend over the shoulder and be free. You'll find the stock needs to be shorter than required for the classic clay-bird or bird-hunting shooting stance. It's harder to reach the fore end, so the gun needs to be shorter.

With the patrol carbine, adjust the stock for the proper length and assume the same consistent stance that was taken with handgun and shotgun. In fact, it's the same stance you take to struggle with a suspect!

Keeping the patrol carbine mounted, muzzle depressed, move forward. Keep those knees bent and the shoulders forward of the waist. First, roll the

Figure 10.6 Consistent stance goes a long way toward being able to fight with whatever you have. Retired SWAT cop and noted writer Gary Johnston demonstrates the consistent stance with the S&W M&P15 rifle.

steps heel to toe. Try it again using "step and drag." The lead foot steps out, the rear foot is pulled up to maintain the stance.

This stance works for fighting, shooting, and moving. It's the power stance.

Power Stance

Have your hands up in front, above the waist, and no higher than shoulder level. One foot leads, usually the left though it really doesn't matter. The other foot is about your shoulders' width from the lead foot. Knees are bent, lowering your center of gravity. Your shoulders are ahead of your waist, less than for shooting a hard-kicking, Express-slug loaded shotgun. It's important not to bend a long way unless you're controlling recoil for fast, follow-up shots.

The feet are pointed with toes toward the target—whether shooting or interviewing. Your hands may be used; you may be jotting notes of a field interview into a small notepad or you may be supporting the elbow of one arm with one hand, while the supported hand is stroking your chin while you listen intently to the subject's words. For people of my era, that "arm-supported" stance is referred to as the "Jack Benny" stance. If you don't know what that means, chat with someone whose hair is gray.

From this stance, we can deflect, grab and grasp, block, strike, move, sweep, and disengage—and we can shoot if needed. The power stance is flexible. Further, power can be generated from the stance.

The format is such that we use the body to strike, when a strike is called for. We don't strike with a hand or a club—the hand or the club is simply the instrument, and the body provides the power.

Consider hitting a golf ball. If you simply move your arms enough to allow the club to strike through the ball, the drive will be short. Take the club back over the shoulders while winding the body up in that line. You are "cocking" the club like the hammer on a Colt Model P. Once the hammer is locked by the sear, the sear trips—that is, you begin your drive by unwinding the body in the direction of the club's travel. Drive the head of the club through the golf ball and back up, twisting the body in the direction of the green. You've just added a lot of yards to your drive. The power came from proper use of your body.

Gun Retention

Though the story is old now, it's as relevant today as ever. The Kansas City (Missouri) Police Department hired a judo player to teach physical skills in their academy. This institution wasn't only a means to train newly hired officers but served as an in-service training model as well. In 1975, a number of Kansas City officers had gotten into struggles and lost their handguns. One was disarmed twice and another was shot to death with his own gun.

The KCPD administration was alarmed and asked their physical skills trainer to come up with a way for officers to hang onto their guns.

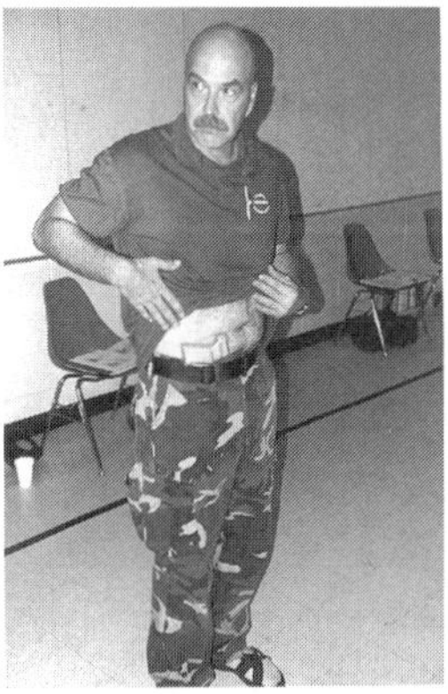

Figure 10.7 We don't always use holsters—ask your narcs or off-duty personnel—even though we need to. This trainer slipped a training gun in his waistband.

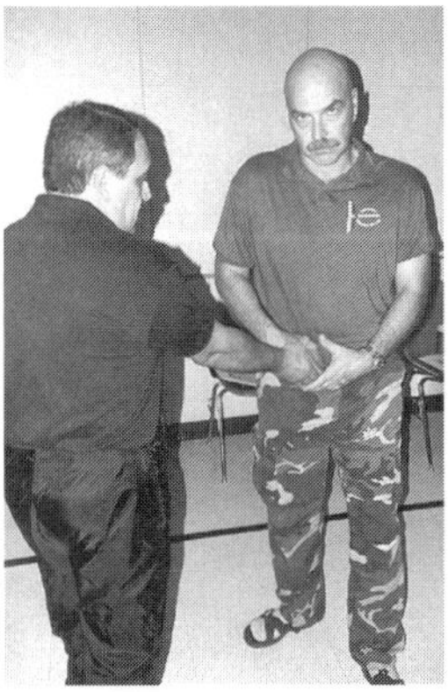

Figure 10.8 The bad guy found the gun and made a grab for it. He grabs and the officer grabs in return, securing the handgun.

James W. Lindell is a wiry, flexible, and quick individual. As a youngster, he was a member of the U.S. Marine Corps and served in a police action in Korea. When he was faced with arriving at a gun retention course, he went at it with grim determination. By 1976, the program was ready and officers got the training.

As it's taught today, the Handgun/Long Gun Retention and Disarming System is a comprehensive, practical, and functional method for dealing with this deadly threat. It requires a moderate investment in defensive tactics training, which is covered in the two-day gun retention instructor's class.

Figure 10.9 After stepping to the outside of the attacker's arm and turning back into him, the officer executes a strike to the outstretched arm.

Figure 10.10 Our erstwhile cop put on a fanny pack and a thief made a grab for it. Same situation—first secure the offender's hand to the pack.

Figure 10.11 Step through him to the outside of the reaching arm and turn into it. Notice the cop's arm is cocked to strike.

Figure 10.12 When he strikes, he goes through the arm all the way up to shoulder level, affecting a release of the crook's grasp on the fanny pack.

An understanding of the function of the handgun and long gun is handy because on the street we're fighting over a real gun. Slides can be forced out of battery, a magazine can get dumped, or a weapon might otherwise reach a stage of unreliability that needs to get remediated quickly.

The basis of Lindell's program is the three-step system of handgun retention: secure, position, and release. When someone grabs an officer's handgun—holstered or drawn—the first step is to secure the gun. When holstered, that's accomplished by a couple of different grips, one from the front and the other from the back. The officer gets into a position of advantage and, from that position, effects the release of the attacker's grasp on the handgun.

I've had people tell me that Lindell's system is too complicated. The quote, I believe, was "Keep it simple, stupid!" But attempts to disarm a police officer aren't always simple and we're not stupid.

The gun grab can occur on a holstered or drawn handgun—the fact is, 50% or more of gun-grab attempts are made on a drawn handgun. It can be your patrol rifle that gets grabbed. Someone could bring his or her own gun and "get the drop," holding you at gunpoint. It's not simple to develop a plan for every contingency.

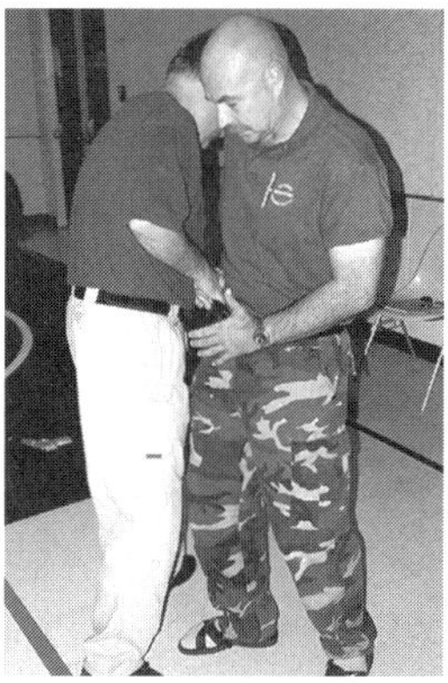

Figure 10.13 Most people don't reach way out to steal, they come in close—setting up another release method.

"Well, if someone grabs my gun, I'll just shoot him!" I've heard. But if the offender is able to seize your handgun, what do you have to shoot him *with*? Besides, can you shoot everyone who clutches at your handgun?

Gun grabs are, without doubt, deadly force situations. If an officer gets a single handcuff on an arrestee who says, "I'm going to get your gun and blow your brains out," as he spins and strikes, I would suggest that it is clearly a situation of assaultive resistance with life-threatening potential.

A friend got a call for service to the Kansas Neurological Institute, a custodial hospital setting for around 300 children afflicted with various mental illness and retardation issues. The uniformed officer arrived to take a report and he was immediately surrounded by children. They came right in on him, fascinated by his accoutrements of office—including his holstered handgun, which was suddenly and strongly grabbed by a number of little hands. That is not the time I would recommend a deadly force response.

Lindell also developed a system of retaining the long gun—MP5, M4, shotgun, or whatever you have, as well as its mirror-image for disarming someone close to you who has a long gun.

Successful gun-grab attempts plummeted in the years following adoption of the Lindell Handgun/Long Gun Retention and Disarming System. World-class firearms trainer Massad Ayoob said he believes that Lindell's system has saved more people than soft body armor has—and body armor has saved many.

Companies like Safariland have been working on the security holster for many years and have made the most secure holsters in history. BlackHawk! CQC has followed, as have others, in making security holsters an easily obtained standard for law enforcement gear.

Security holsters and armor help, but every peace officer needs gun retention training. I'm stuck on Jim Lindell's system. It's the one I know.

The prime directive in gun retention training is to only use cast, nonfiring guns with no moving parts. Never, ever use a real gun. Avoid the FX-style gun or factory-made nonfiring versions of the real thing. By touch, they can't be immediately identified as models and a real one can slip into the room after a break.

Speaking of breaks, a safety check of no guns, knives, and aerosols must be done at every return to class.

Where do you get the fake guns? There are a number of vendors. One of the highest quality makers of molded guns is Ring's (check http://www.blueguns.com/). Made of polyurethane, they are resistant to impacts. I don't know how good they are for Lindell's style of gun retention training. It gets intense and I'm waiting for a trigger guard to break.

When doing gun retention training, I use Lindell's training guns. Made from case aluminum, they are weighty. I've never seen one break. That said, Ring's has a huge collection of different models of guns. I use Ring's for

Figure 10.14 This police holster is the Safariland ALS. Quick to resecure after having reholstered, it's also quick on the draw and scores high in weapon retention.

holster work in nonfiring environments and in front of classes. I use Lindell's for all the hands-on stuff as long as I can find one to fit the holster we're using—which is nearly all the time. (For more information, contact http://www.nletc.com/.)

Figure 10.15 This is the BlackHawk! CQC Serpa holster. Also quick to resecure when holstering, this model is a concealable holster with a retention feature.

Figure 10.16 Ring's training guns come in a variety of models, some that aren't made by NLETC/Jim Lindell. Watch for breakage when the training gets heavy.

Figure 10.17 The Lindell training gun is made of cast aluminum, carefully rounded. The dark gun under it is a Ring's training gun—not as durable as Lindell's but good for holster training and to apply LaserGrips to.

A Firearms Instructor in Defensive Tactics Land

In 1995, after 12 years as a firearms instructor, I was tasked with attending the instructor class in gun retention from Lindell's National Law Enforcement Training Center in Kansas City, Missouri. That was 17 years after I had graduated from the academy. The only defensive tactics class I'd had since was Monadnock's PR-24 baton-user class and that was in 1986. I went to Kansas City having no idea what I was doing.

They talked in funny, non-gun terms, like "Lower your center," "Take his center," and "This is like the Number Two wristlock." I had no experience to prepare me for this training.

On top of that, I had to return to my department and give the eight-hour postacademy user class to 103 officers—after an instructor class of just two days. Using the Lindell System, we successfully trained 103 officers in the techniques. I went back the next year and took Lindell's Control and Defensive Tactics Instructor class, among other classes, which filled in lots of blanks from my first trip to Kansas City. Except for the summer I lost my father, I've been back to Kansas City every year.

A year after my first gun retention class, I had a magazine article assignment to go to a handgun manufacturer's training unit and take a couple of weeks of tactical and instructor training from them. They did a "weapons retention" section that required heavy-duty work gloves and real guns—something I never recommend and would not allow on my place. As this was a SWAT-style class, everything was geared toward moving forward and not stopping—unless someone grabbed your drawn handgun. This required a step back for one of their responses.

I don't sharp-shoot instructors in front of other students, but I had to share the forearm leverage release with them—it went with their "keep moving" philosophy. I don't believe they adopted it, but it's a great technique when someone grabs your handgun with two hands.

As a nondefensive tactics firearms instructor, I have certified gun retention instructors for the past six or so years at Kansas City. It's been my privilege to do so.

The Bridge

Becoming a gun retention instructor is the natural bridge from firearms instruction to defensive tactics. It's the bridge I took and it's a "best fit." It happens that having defensive tactics types of people move from their field to firearms is best accomplished by stepping across the gun retention bridge.

Gun retention and disarming is critical training for everyone who carries a gun. It has good crossover into retaining other property you don't want to lose. It enhances mind-set. Having people try to grab that nonfiring training gun from you about 200 times in a couple of days does a lot to teach you what you should be looking for.

Training in the Lindell System is broadly available across the United States and in several venues overseas. For more information, contact the National Law Enforcement Training Center, 3238 Gillham Road, Kansas City, MO 64109; 800-445-0857; http://www.nletc.com/index.php. That's the place to get the training guns, too.

Figure 10.18 The gun grab is never good. This offender (wearing the protective apparel) is hurled in the air as the victim-officer retains his drawn handgun.

The Dance: Bringing the Street to the Range 11

Dynamics

The square range is the place to learn essential skills. The ability to hit a mark at various distances and from various positions is learned here. Sight picture and sight alignment are reinforced here. The basics of learning firearms are born here.

That said, it's a very artificial place. There are rules here. A number of otherwise great instructors teach students that the square range is the place where "All guns have to be unloaded. Don't think, just do what I tell you. Don't move from that spot—moving with loaded guns is dangerous."

Is that the street? Do we want them to wander about with empty guns? Is it the job of the peace officer not to think with gun in hand? Do we want them to stand stock still when they are under fire? If these things are unsafe on the range, they have to be horribly dangerous in the world. If these things are unsafe on the range, where can we practice to face life on the street?

Is there a way to blend the range and the street? Can we make live-fire training more realistic without throwing safety out the window?

Basics

To start with, everyone has to have his or her basic skills set together. I don't begin with "shooting from unconventional positions," "shooting on the move," and "one-hand manipulation drills." I begin with a simple exam to see where we are.

The International Association of Law Enforcement Firearms Instructors (IALEFI) does an annual seminar every year. They get new attendees at each seminar—mostly from around the United States but with a few members from overseas. We can't know what each of them brings to the table without seeing them work.

All new attendees have to do the IALEFI safety check. Using a firearm, a magazine, and a holster, they have to demonstrate some basic skills. These include loading, unloading, drawing, reholstering, and some pivots and

Figure 11.1 The standards are shot individually, so the instructor is able to later testify as to an individual's performance. It's collecting evidence for a case that's yet to be filed.

turns. Each skill is demonstrated before the new attendees perform it. This way we have some expectation that a new attendee won't have an event-ending accident based on not being up to speed.

All of the IALEFI presenters keep careful track of the members in their presentations and try to ensure they don't go faster than the troops can go. In Chapter 4, we discussed the constantly reborn shooter—that individual who comes to the range, learns after a fashion, and marginally "passes." By the next trip to the range, our hero has "forgotten" every bit of progress we made in the previous trip. Is this someone who should do the safety check?

If I'm doing a firearms in-service class or a seminar, we'll start with rules of the road and a warm-up. That warm-up is time for me to evaluate what I've got to work with and gives me an idea of how fast we can go. It's not objective—there's no baseline standard, though I may lightly customize the warm-up based on what I expect we'll be doing during the program.

At my last agency, we'd begun a "firearms standards drill." Discussed in Chapter 8, the standards combine a bit of basic skills, remarkably like the IALEFI Safety Check and the Kansas Law Enforcement Training Center Basic Standards, but different in some ways from each. The standards drill lets them "see and do," perfecting their own performance. It's also a good warm-up. They can watch me shoot the standards, as we discuss them. Then they perform them individually, for the record.

Figure 11.2 The timer can be used as your people get used to the standards to collect time data. This helps to show how "smooth equals fast." Note the notebook in the leg pocket of the instructor's trousers.

The standards drill is passed at 100% in performance with 100% hits. Like the qualification, a student doing the standards exercises is "paying the bills," doing something someone else requires of them. Passing the standards and the state-mandated qualification means you are allowed to work.

But the standards drill is a good warm-up and it allows students to self-remediate.

Tactical Foundation

Basically, identify everything we do or are expected to do in the square range environment. Make a list. Examine gunfight after-action reports. Most agencies are too small to have a significant database, so use information from the larger agencies. Look at the dynamics of the fight. Use information from the FBI Incident-Based Reporting System, including the Officers Killed and Assaulted Summaries and the books that are based on those data.

Put the various issues in a context. What can we do on the square range to prepare them for the battle? Where are the differences and how can we bring the street to the range? Do a lesson plan and drill development sheet for each aspect you find. At the end, you'll have more training than you can deliver in a career.

For basic training, the square range is where we learn to shoot. In in-service, we use the square range to learn how to *fight*. There's a difference.

Problem: Decision Making

The easiest decision-making method is also the hardest: Simulations are costly, require their own unique safety regulation, take lots of time and lots of personnel, and require a new nonrange location. They are also critical to an officer's success in the world.

But if you need to do decision-making live-fire training and for administrative reasons can't do simulations right now, you can still deliver the goods on the square range. One agency had a range with a turning target system. They scheduled a range training day. When officers arrived, during their shifts, they had to check in at the range house. After checking in and gearing up, a range officer took out one officer at a time. The targets, at rest, faced the north side of the range. Trainees had to approach the sound end of the range. At the 7-yard line, large wooden barricades had been set up. These limited the officer's view of the target line to only the target he or she had to his or her immediate front.

When the targets were made to turn, they couldn't isolate and only turn one at a time and hence were physical obstructions to limit the trainees' ability to see the upcoming targets. The range officer had the trainee step into the first firing box and face the target line. On signal, the target faced the shooter but only for three seconds. During that time, the trainee had to (1) identify a threat and (2) take the appropriate action. If it was move, draw, and verbalize, so be it. If it was shoot to stop, the trainee had a short time to accomplish the task.

The targets were "photo" targets, not blank silhouettes. Some had guns or a knife, while others had empty hands or maybe a badge. On targets that "required shooting," the hits had to be in time and on target. This doesn't take the place of simulations but it beat facing a blank silhouette and instructions to "Fire 12 rounds in 25 seconds." If you don't have turning targets, you can turn the officers while you change the target identifiers.

One enterprising trainer bought Airsoft guns and supplemented them with old paintball guns the SWAT unit had used in training. Using the rules in the simulations chapter (see Chapter 12), he did interactive force-on-force training.

Another brought spray paint to the range and used his steel targets. For that exercise, the fire commands were "red," "blue," "white," or combinations of these. Among the lessons learned were threat discrimination, accuracy, and speed. To increase speed, we would duplicate the range setup. This gave us two lanes and we could have shooter versus shooter contests. The one who put a pair of hits on his or her target before the other could was the winner.

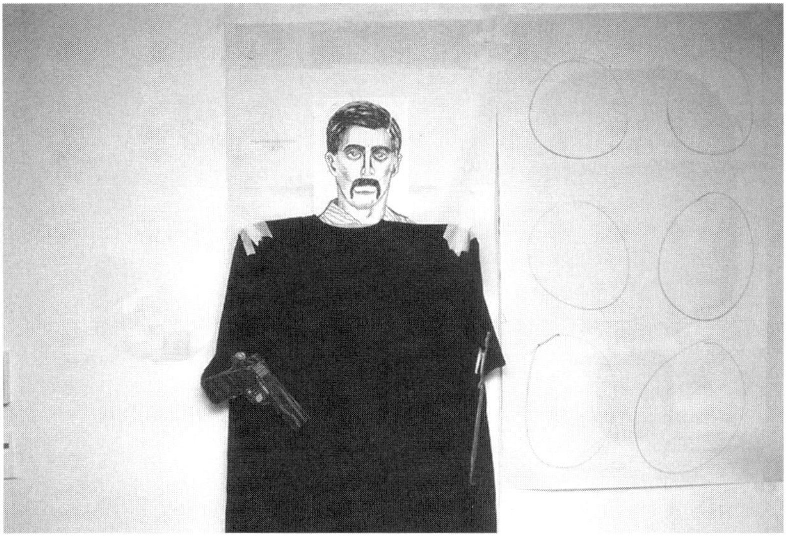

Figure 11.3 Targets can be "dressed" to prevent aiming at a scoring ring. Note the "pistol" cutout prop. This as easily could be a knife, badge, or empty hand.

When the instructor had a pair of shooters up and gave the commands, "Blue-blue-red!" there was a great deal of scrambling.

The great thing about steel targets is that we need to be 10-plus yards away to minimize injuries due to backsplatter. Another great thing is that

Figure 11.4 These knock-down targets wear shirts of different colors, allowing decision making based on the call of a color by the instructor.

Figure 11.5 Looking at the target causes misses, as demonstrated here.

people tend to want to see their bullets hit the target. Most people have trouble hitting a steel target 10 yards away when using a target focus.

Our shooters would hit way low due to the phenomenon of eye sprints, when a shooter uses a front sight focus, presses through the trigger and, at the break of the shot, immediately looks up over the gun at the steel target.

Figure 11.6 Four targets and two shooters can make this a competitive exercise.

Figure 11.7 Metal targets require some distance for safety and reinforce front sight focus.

Figure 11.8 For a competitive exercise, split the plate rack between two shooters or go by time to clear the rack; the officer with the shortest time is the winner.

Figure 11.9 "Behind the Curve": One shooter is the attacker and the other is defender. The defender watches the attacker. When the attacker goes for his gun, the defender goes for his. The attacker shoots the target to his front—the defender shoots at his own target. Only hits count, but the attempt is to drive speed of the draw.

The problem with target focus on steel is that you don't hit the target. The ones who make the occasional hit don't realize it's a lucky hit and they keep trying to "catch lighting in a bottle."

Problem: Increasing Speed of the First Hit from the Holster

The way ranges are often run is that a line of shooters stand shoulder-to-shoulder facing a line of targets. The targets turn or another signal is given to fire. They all shoot at one time and stop shooting at one time. This creates problems for thinking, moving fighters. It minimizes range administration and allegedly makes the range "safer."

The real signal to start shooting might be seeing a person whom we suspect is armed make a sudden move, as if moving to draw that gun. When do we see that move on the range? Is this a movement our shooters can even recognize?

Have two shooters stand side-by-side, with one as the designated attacker. It's that individual's job to make the sudden, furtive movement that starts a fight. The other shooter is watching our designated attacker from the side. Both are armed with holstered and secured pistols.

Figure 11.10 These students shot nearly simultaneously, showing that their skill was on the increase.

At some point, the attacker will draw and put a hit in the center of a target to his or her front. The other shooter sees the movement and, as quickly as possible, draws and puts a hit into his or her own target. The object is to make reaction beat action.

Is that possible? We've had some Pyrrhic victories where the hits are nearly simultaneous—after practice. We've often used this as a prelude to movement on the range. In any event, each of the pair of shooters plays the attacker and the defender roles. Practice is continued until speed of draw is optimal. The competitive drive helps move shooters along.

I was asked if I was concerned that someone would draw and fire based simply on a subject's movement. That scenario lacks a context. Peace officers have no situations on the street that lack context with the exception of a random ambush.

This drill requires no special equipment or range setup. It's invaluable.

Problem: Unconventional Positions and Cover

I've been to many ranges and a common staple is an open plain of 50-plus yards in front of an impact berm. Mostly that open plain is unblemished with furniture, cars, kids' toys, utility poles, fire hydrants, and other artifacts of recent human activity. This has little relationship to the battlefield environment that peace officers face.

Figure 11.11 To increase pressure, have the defender move laterally as the attacker moves to draw.

It's always better to have something between you and gunfire than it is to have nothing in between but air. It is also reasonable to conclude that officers

Figure 11.12 "Dress" the range. This range has a pair of wooden barricades for use of a moving target. There are steel targets in place as well as a car and mailboxes for cover items.

Figure 11.13 An array of targets can be used for decision making. Note that one target is armed, the other is showing hands. The poppers are different colors, allowing for a "color call" for a hit.

won't seek cover on the street if their only shooting experience has been in the open on a range. Seeking cover has to be a learned response. It isn't instinctive.

To ensure that officers will seek cover during the battle, it's helpful to make them shoot from behind simulated cover items at every opportunity. This is made more effective by making them use cover effectively. The problem with effectively using items of cover and concealment out in the world is often that item isn't a vertical, bulletproof wall. Sometimes it is a round tree or utility pole. Other times, it could be a car—imperfect as those can be in terms of being "real cover."

Our items of simulated cover on a range shouldn't always be a board protruding vertically from the ground. Making the stair-step barricade is one way to enforce low cover usage. Getting one or more old fireplugs from Public Works to put out on the range makes for another good training aid.

The range is usually level. What if you are on uneven ground? We normally shoot without being surrounded by walls or the ground, or under a vehicle. How are those positions different? Most shooting ranges have trainees standing up, in the open, and standing still while they shoot. What if the officer is seated and, for one reason or another, can't get up to engage the threat?

We have our people shoot with two hands on the handgun. I remember saying, "The only reason you shoot a pistol with two hands is that you don't have three," and thinking I was clever. I've since found that surprised officers with extreme close-range threats shoot one-handed. It's also been brought to

Figure 11.14 Why shoot with one hand? The other hand could be busy or it could be injured.

my attention that cop killers nearly always shoot one-handed. They wouldn't be called "cop killers" if they hadn't killed cops, so that indicates some success on their part.

That said, I prefer for trainees to have two hands on the gun. The fact is that they may not and we have to train for that eventuality. They may have

Figure 11.15 Draw and fire, one-handed. The shooter in the foreground is using a subcompact pistol—the one he might have when the fight starts.

Figure 11.16 If you're down or disabled, you have to use the hand you have left. This shooter uses "cover" in the form of a chair.

to shoot with the "wrong hand" in the fight, as their primary hand could be damaged. This leads to Jim Cirillo's Down and Disabled Officer (DDO) Program.

Being down or disabled brings up another dimension to the unconventional position shooting experience. Jim began the program after an officer was shot down but still alive and still capable of fighting back. According to witnesses, he didn't fight back but tried to surrender to his attackers. Never

Figure 11.17 Ever reload upside down? The time to learn is not in a fight.

Figure 11.18 Stance is where you end up when shots are fired. In this case, the officer was knocked down (simulated) and has to respond to a deadly threat.

having prepared for the eventuality that he'd have to fight from a down and partly disabled status, he was shot dead while he pleaded for his life.

Jim couldn't let this stand. When last I checked, elements of his DDO class were still taught at the Federal Law Enforcement Training Center.

Figure 11.19 Mix and match: this downed officer course has graphic photo targets that are covered by shirts.

Figure 11.20 Shooting with the less dominant hand is a critical skill for officer survival.

Figure 11.21 Derived from a real case, Cirillo put together a down-and-disabled officer course of fire.

Figure 11.22 How do you reload if you only have one hand? It's good to get that arranged in training. It's hard to learn during a gunfight.

Officers shoot from supine positions between their feet and knees—the location in front of the muzzle making old-fashioned range officers weak-kneed to observe. They shoot from the fetal position on either side. They shoot from supine back overhead to a target "standing over them" over their heads.

A concern is the height of the berm. Before doing such drills, check to ensure that gunfire won't go over the backstop. If your range backstop is too short, use Airsoft guns but understand that they won't feel the special way the gun recoils from that position. And officers won't feel the back blast reflected from the ground.

Another thing to do is to have the guns grounded before the officers are grounded and in position. This way, they can more easily control the muzzles.

Figure 11.23 The chair drill, as devised by Clive Shepherd, begins on a relaxed note.

Students should be nervous in this training; it's not a pleasant prospect to have happen on the street to shoot over and past your legs.

Watch those muzzles!

Chairs

Nonmetal plastic chairs are handy to have on the range. If you only have metal chairs, understand that they can get shot—anything that's ahead of the shooters can get shot. A bullet hole in a metal chair leaves a sharp edge. Be prepared to dress it and tape it.

Why the discussion about chairs? The chair drill helps cover a lot of the concerns of the previous section. Each shooter has a chair. It'll be a chair for them to sit on, to step on, to shoot under, and to hold while shooting—or not.

An invention of tactical shooting impresario Clive Shepherd, the chair drill was a staple of his training classes. By using the chair for simulated cover, shooting over it and to either side of it—even under it and feeling the blast—the chair becomes a multiuse training aid. Trainees have to draw and shoot from seated positions, sitting on the chair the way it was designed, sitting with the chair back forward toward their target and with knees on either side of the chair back. Note: Officers need to have learned the safety circle

Figure 11.24 When the shooting command is delivered, it's time to go to work.

and to have inculcated it in their psyches to do this safely. Also, speed isn't the point here—it's experiential. Don't use stop watches on this drill!

Shooters will fire with the right foot on the chair, with both feet on the chair (unsteady as that is), and with the left foot up and on the chair.

After 50 rounds and about 15 minutes on a single target, a large number of training points are made and reinforced.

Figure 11.25 Sometimes you will be seated facing away from a potential threat. You still have to respond.

Figure 11.26 One response is the lazy shooter's way—handy if you are a right-handed shooter.

Range World

Notice that we haven't talked about spending lots of money on special target systems, live-fire shooting houses, or other gear. We have spent a little time on some drills—and this is the tip of the iceberg. Many who read this book already have good ideas on making range training street relevant.

Figure 11.27 On the command to get two hands on the gun, we get this result.

Figure 11.28 They get up to shoot.

If this has whetted your appetite, take an NRA Instructor Development School. The current classes have more information along the lines of tactical range training on a budget. For more information, go to http://www.nrahq.org/law/training/training.asp.

For those who are current or would like exposure to a broader range of instructors, check out the IALEFI Annual Training Conference. Join IALEFI and participate. Their magazine (*Firearms Instructor*) alone is worth

Figure 11.29 Facing uprange is designed to make the traditional firearms instructor shiver. It's best to have a command of the safety circle before this stage.

Figure 11.30 Shooters won't always be on even ground, as shown here.

the price of membership. For membership and conference information, take a look at http://www.ialefi.com/.

Figure 11.31 Sometimes shooters are on unsteady ground.

Figure 11.32 Having fired from elevation, it's time to look around for other potential threats.

Figure 11.33 What happens if you are holding a chair in your gun hand?

Figure 11.34 Dropping behind a chair to fight.

Figure 11.35 Do you fire seated or move? It's the shooter's problem to solve.

Figure 11.36 Sometimes we can't extend the gun to fire. It's important to try this on a range first. Note that the slide hits the shooter's chest, tying the gun up.

Figure 11.37 If the shotgun quit shooting, is it empty or is there something else wrong? It doesn't matter—transition to the pistol and continue to march.

Simulations: Lessons Learned

12

Gunfight Training

Shooting isn't gunfighting, and learning to shoot a gun is not learning all the things that are necessary to winning the fight. Shooting is a mechanical skill, often learned in the closed environment of the square range.

Motor skills trainers will tell you that acquiring closed skills sets, while essential to getting a foundation in the discipline, is only part of the learning process. In the old, old days, the most training an aspiring fighter might get would be shooting at cans and rocks on the outskirts of town. In the dawn of police firearms carry and qualification, the targets were circular with a black center (the "bull's-eye"). Rounds were fired at slow, timed, and "rapid fire" cadences all while using one hand only to control the gun.

As time went on, there was a drive to make it more realistic, hence the use of humanoid silhouettes as targets. While this wasn't a terrible move, it didn't "close the circle."

Eventually, agencies like the NYPD started loading primed .38 cases with wet cotton balls and did "man-on-man" scenario-based training. It was there that the training community determined that our lousy hit ratio on the street was directly related to what we *cannot* learn on the square range.

In the last decade of the 20th century, the use of interactive gunfight simulations in police training were all but required in certain parts of the United States. Paintball guns and marking cartridges had already been in use and lessons were being quickly—and sometimes tragically—learned.

Training Safety

We discussed the disparity in force training earlier in this volume. This "diversity" created more trouble than it solved.

Part of our problem is precisely because of that self-imposed categorization of trainers: we had firearms instructors who were different from the defensive tactics instructors who were sometimes different from the baton instructors and the chemical aerosol instructors. Firearms instructors had

Figure 12.1 Simulations include outdoor situations, shown here, with shoot–no shoot targets. There's no real interaction here and the targets seldom, if ever, move.

their students shoot because shooting is what you do at the range. Often there was simple marksmanship training. On other facilities, there would be cover drills, shooting on the move and with multiple targets. In any case, there was no physical contact and usually no de-escalation.

When it came time to do gun retention training, there was a bridge between the "gun guys" and the "mat room guys." This caused some interrelationship that in turn caused some rethinking of the problem. Forward-looking outfits had used the cotton-ball scam. Later the popular paintball sport appeared and it was taken into police gunfight training.

It quickly became apparent that protective apparel was the order of the day. This was hot and uncomfortable, but somewhat comforting when you got hit. Many officers, when hit with a .68 caliber paintball, simply gave up. "Aw, you got me" was an all-too-common refrain. Some of us instructed role-players to continue to shoot to make them fight.

The problems with paintballs added up. The guns weren't similar to duty guns and didn't fit the holsters. If the temperature was too low, paintballs turned into *pain* balls, a congealed mess that hit like ball bearings. Sometimes the players got too close, just like in real life, with resulting injuries.

When we went to guns that fit the holsters and looked just like our duty guns, they were often duty guns converted to fire-marking cartridges.

Insufficient planning and site security led to tragic cases where officers came into a training scenario with real guns loaded with *real* ammo. Tragedy resulted again and again.

This wasn't a problem with the equipment. Like most of our problems, they were training issues. One can't buy one's way out of training issues. A concerned industry and training community came together to find ways to ensure training safety and a sterile training site.

The Gunsite Way

There are a number of ways to ensure a sterile environment. Outstanding membership organizations like the National Tactical Officers Association and the International Association of Law Enforcement Firearms Instructors have moved quickly to address the issue in an industry-wide fashion.

This chapter isn't intended to demonstrate *the* way to make gunfight simulation training safe, but to show *one* way it has been done. To do that, we'll look at one of the world's foremost training venues: Gunsite Academy of Paulden, Arizona.

As early in the handgun training line as the 350 pistol class, students are exposed to gunfight simulations. In the 250 and again in the 350, students begin work in the classroom and the square range. Fundamentals are taught, polished, and reinforced. Students then move to live-fire outdoor and indoor simulators.

In the Arizona high desert, there is a lot of room for outdoor simulators like "the Wash." Students learn how to approach corners, identify threats, and formulate responses.

In the indoor simulators, which are live-fire shooting houses, photo-targets are placed to make demands on the students' judgment skills. Their abilities to move, shoot, and communicate are stretched. They have to deal with corners, discern "people" in the room, determine if a threat exists, and respond appropriately.

All work in simulators is done with a coach following close behind. The coach acts as role-player, the voice of the target, and watches performance with a critical eye.

When the simulators are done, the challenge remaining is the Simunitions® exercise. This is an interactive experience with living, breathing opponents. The difference from other forms of role-play is that the participants are armed with Simunitions FX marking cartridge-enabled guns.

Guns so enabled are incapable of taking live, lethal ammunition. Otherwise the guns are the same as they were. Unfortunately, real guns are going to be seen in the Sims exercise. How do you ensure that no lethal instruments are introduced? Law enforcement agencies have found out that strict security

Figure 12.2 Indoor simulators are a good way to move to interactive simulations. Here, a student prepares to enter a shoothouse under the watchful eye of the instructor.

Figure 12.3 Door approaches vary, but the objective is to get out of that doorway quickly.

Figure 12.4 A shooter approaches a blind corner in a room.

is needed. Such knowledge has been gained through the loss of life of participants. At Gunsite, there is a strict protocol in place.

Students are prepped to understand that *no* metal items, objects, or clothing items will be allowed in the training site. They are given a sterile area in which they are checked for weapons. That area is guarded the entire time the Sims exercises are ongoing. If a student has to go to the head, he or she is searched again upon return.

Students remove all metal items on their own. Then they are checked with a metal detector wand. If there is a metal reading, it can lead to a pat down for a weapon. No knives are allowed. Obviously, no guns are allowed either.

Protective headgear is issued. Shooting glasses must be worn under the protective mask to ensure double protection of the eyes. This is no place to cut corners!

There is a padded wrap to go around the neck, and armor is issued. While not "bullet-proof," the armor minimizes the discomfort that accompanies being shot by the Simunitions FX cartridge. The armor extends down far enough to protect the groin. Gloves are also available.

All guns are provided. When I went to Gunsite in 2002, I was issued a Glock 17T blue-frame gun that takes *only* Simunitions FX rounds. They also

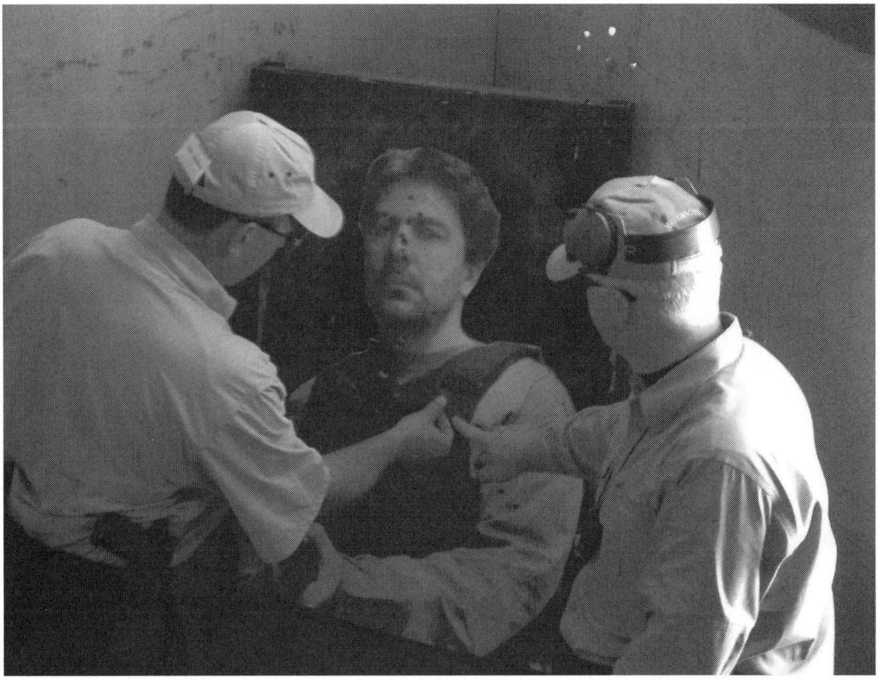

Figure 12.5 Use of nonhuman targets in a shoothouse helps decision making but is no match for a living, moving, thinking opponent.

had an AR-15 set up to take Sims rounds. In 2003, their stock included a shotgun modified to take the FX cartridge and some 1911s that were so modified.

Gunsite provided a nylon belt and a blue Kydex holster made by Sidearmor. I was in an armed robbery scenario and shot it out with the robbery suspect and a seeded backup. I was surprised how quickly I got the gun out and on target. Like the G17T Sims gun's frame, the Sidearmor holster is made in blue. This commonality in "safe" colors is an added security step.

Lessons Learned

Going through a Sims exercise with high-speed, low-drag fellow instructors and trainees can be very instructive. I interviewed several of the guys I went through the program with and came away with lessons that were as important for the street as they were instructional in the Sims environment.

Operator No. 1: One worthy fighter elected not to go where it was "logical" to go. He was taken into a workplace violence situation that he didn't want to go into in the first place. When he didn't move down a hallway but instead went to a door short of the apparent source of the trouble, he was told

Figure 12.6 Specialized guns are needed for interactive training. The Glock, 1911, Remington 870, and pair of AR-15 rifles are converted to use Simunitions FX marking cartridges.

that the door didn't go anywhere. He pulled it open anyway, came in behind the scenario, and surprised the violator, settling the confrontation. He did the unexpected and came away the victor.

Lesson: Take the initiative and do the unexpected. The offender is usually known for this, but we are not. Feel free to think outside the box. Interactive simulations exercises are *open* skills sets, not the closed environment skills of the range. Doing the unexpected has long been a part of officer survival training. Be predictably unpredictable. Take the long way or the hard way to a scene. You might catch them looking the other way.

Make a passenger side approach on a nighttime car stop. Make them wonder why.

Operator No. 2: Another colleague was set upon by an obviously out-of-control individual. He armed himself and issued verbal warnings that were specific to the situation. The violator was acting in a threatening fashion but no gun was immediately apparent.

Hollow bluffs don't work. Our hero ordered the wild role-player out of the building and offered deadly force—he told the player that he would be shot in a part of his body that had no protection. By doing this, ownership of the force decision was transferred to the intruder. The intruder, according to

Figure 12.7 This Glock 17T is made from the factory to shoot nothing but FX marking cartridges.

script, went for his hidden handgun. The warning was followed by the exact application of the force offered, as soon as it became apparent that the role-player was armed. That Sims round hurt!

The lesson here is this: when you have an uncooperative suspect—as we never do on the square range, but always seem to have on the street—tell them what they have to do and offer a force consequence. "See this Taser? Get on the ground! Now!" If he's still resisting and that level of force is appropriate to the situation, follow through.

Operator No. 3: One other classmate had one piece of advice: Look! He watched everyone and didn't prejudge the players. He was rewarded by seeing a poorly concealed handgun and was able to surprise the role-players in the scenario.

Lesson: The visual frisk is an important element in threat evaluation. Also, watch for mannerisms, such as the offender touching his waistband, hidden by a cover garment. Most bad guys don't use holsters and often "feel" to ensure their hidden weapon is still there.

Operator No. 4: Finally, a renowned trainer proved the rule that decisive, aggressive action can win the day. He was confronted with multiple armed opponents. Moving quickly and shooting on the move, he scored hits on every "criminal" in the scenario. Only one got a shot off and that round hit empty clothing without striking the trainer's body.

Figure 12.8 The slide is marked, indicating that the gun is built for simulations only.

Equipment

Training demands from the law enforcement arena caused the development of the Glock 17T training pistols. The Glock 17T is fabricated in a straight blow-back system to ensure function with the FX marking cartridge. The blue pistol frame is instantly recognized as a dedicated training gun.

The round that the Glock 17T 9mmFX is designed to fire is the Simunitions color-marking cartridge. This is an asset for interactive simulations training.

The 17T is also very handy for shooting drills when a shooting range is unavailable or has a short backstop. For example, the Topeka (Kansas) Police Department sometimes has to do their pepper spray training course in a parking lot. Their guns are Glocks modified to use FX cartridges. During the class, students are exposed to OC spray and have to fight. At some point in the exercise, the contaminated student has to shoot for his or her life. Center hits are required to stop the threat. The FX cartridges aren't as loud as conventional 9mm ammo and the marking pellet goes only a short way.

In a grounded, disabled officer defense training class, Sims guns can be used even at the steep angles that allow fired rounds to miss the impact berm.

Figure 12.9 Gunsite has blue holsters—made by Sidearmor—for their Sims-converted handguns. Note the Garrett metal detector, also used to ensure simulations safety.

The marking pellets fall harmlessly to earth in a short distance, unlike the long distances that a centerfire handgun bullet can travel.

Train the Trainer

Interactive simulations and role-playing are definitely the way to go in gunfight preparation. As already mentioned, safety is an enormous issue, but so is making the simulation work for the students. There are very specific rules to making the best scenario and tightly scripting it to maintain control and ensure a quality product.

As Giles Stock, Gunsite staff instructor, pointed out, the scenario must be winnable. "We could go out, ambush students, and gun them all down," he said. "But that's not the point of the exercise. They *can* win if they don't make mistakes."

And mistakes are pointed out, better ways are demonstrated. You learn in the shoothouse, on the range, and in the mat room so you don't have to learn it in the street when it's for real.

Figure 12.10 After removing all metal objects, each participant is wanded to ensure that no one carries an actual weapon into the simulation training.

An Alternative

Simunitions are expensive. They're also fired in guns that can conceivably fire frangible, nonmarking munitions that can cause serious injury or death if you get the wrong ammo. Without going back to paintball guns that look, feel, handle, and holster like no handgun ever carried by police, is there an alternative?

Cool gas-fired plastic projectiles are used in Airsoft guns. These are model guns that are fired by use of a spring, by "green gas," CO_2 or electrically. The little plastic "BBs" are usually not propelled quickly enough to damage property but you may want to check your "lanes of fire" in the scenario.

We were able to use them almost everywhere, including an office building that was closed for the evening. At the conclusion of festivities, we ran a vacuum cleaner and swept all the plastic pellets up! Unlike Sims, which can wreck wallboard and window glass and leave marks that are nearly impossible to clean up, you can use Airsoft almost everywhere. Check your guns to ensure that nothing gets broken; little things are often used as excuses to stop training efforts.

In spite of their relatively low speed, they do hit hard enough to let the shootee know that their use of cover wasn't optimum!

Figure 12.11 No one is exempt from presimulations inspection. If someone has to go out for a moment and return, the inspection is redone.

Putting It Together

Sgt. Jack Morgan, now retired, put together a day of gunfight simulations for in-service during a recent training year. He'd been working on the students with threat focus shooting. When the simulations day arrived, the students appeared at the range, had a short safety and informational in-briefing, and then disarmed and were searched.

They began with cover drills on the range. Using items of cover, including their stair-step barricades and portable target frames with cardboard, an individual student would try to keep from being shot by a paintball-wielding role-player. They learned about proximity to cover and how to best use it. They went to Simunitions marking cartridges for car stop scenarios and went on to building searches in the dark with Airsoft.

This was a rounded day of training to fight. A full decade before, I had been assigned to prepare three days of in-service. Training Day 1 (TD1) was gun retention and disarming, another subject that requires really disarmed police trainees. TD2 was simulations.

We began with the Bureau of Alcohol, Tobacco, and Firearms (ATF) training tape *Psyche of Survival*. Through interviews with agents who'd been shot in the line of duty and comments by physicians and psychologists, the

Figure 12.12 Gearing up for Sims: The protection of the head and neck are mandatory. Protective apparel over the chest and groin aren't required by everyone, but the smart trainee covers up!

trainees learned that they are quite likely to stay alive after being shot. To do so requires keeping your head in the fight and not giving up. In the film, one agent told his story about how—downed and disabled—he had to kill his attacker, but he lived to tell about it. The lesson was not to give up if you get hurt.

After that, everyone was briefed at the scenario training site and they were disarmed. Protective clothing was the order of the day. We warmed up with the Interactive Hogan's Alley, a hallway that the student had to walk along. Living, breathing, talking "targets" would present in doorways—not in every door, but periodically. Students were told they'd have to give verbal

Figure 12.13 The students learn to stay back from corners and doorways.

Figure 12.14 A trainee gets briefed on a simulation that is about to start.

Figure 12.15 This is what the trainee can't see: the subject in the car already has a gun in hand.

Figure 12.16 Trainees were scored for caution. This one stays with his car and issues verbal direction.

Figure 12.17 Another trainee also stays back and calls out to the offender. This is a good start.

instructions, ask questions, and respond as appropriate. There were a number of "no-shoot" targets. We had one with a "knife" that was only shot by one trainee—over 90% of them never saw the "knife"!

Figure 12.18 Sometimes real offenders go mobile. This one, in a suicide-in-progress situation, approaches the officer with a gun to his own head. Note the officer's position relative to the car and the offender. Care to guess what happened next?

Another target had his hands in his pockets. He was waiting for the verbal instruction "Get your hands out of your pockets!" He had a snubnose revolver in his hand in one of those pockets. He could draw and shoot before the officer holding him at gunpoint could respond!

Alarm Call

The second major scenario was the "crime in progress" call. We'd send in a team acting as if we were giving them time to plan. The scenario started in front of them before even a hasty plan could be made—an armed robber was backing out of the scene of the crime right into them! He'd see them and run and we'd watch to see how many actually chased without a plan.

That never seemed to end well. After that one, you couldn't get a deputy to even come near a scenario without talking it over with a partner!

Gaming

A little simulation goes a long way. It can quickly devolve into a paid game of "cops and robbers." Don't let that happen. Having them interviewed after a scenario is one way of bringing everything back to reality.

We ran a group of recruits through a training scenario on a nearby airbase. I had a video camera that recorded every performance of every recruit on every scenario. One would come in, get a briefing, act out the scenario—which was recorded—and then be sent out to write a report. Another troop came in and got the same scenario and left for report writing. We did this for a number of scenarios.

I collected the reports and the videotapes and turned them over to our detective supervisor. A few days later, we had the recruits on the range. The detective arrived with a box containing reports and video tapes. He took the recruits one by one for interviews. If one of them asked for a lawyer, we had decided, I'd be his lawyer.

Their reports weren't always a reflection of what was seen on video. They had a chance to explain that just as if it had been a real shooting. Afterward, we had a debriefing of the scenarios, the report writing, and the detective interviews. It was a valuable training experience for them, combining decision making in the use of force with shooting skill, with reporting uses of force, and finally being called to account.

Don't let it become a game.

A Unique Environment

There is nothing quite like simulations training to replicate the street. In our rush to replicate the street in training, we inadvertently replicated the danger. The loss of officers to training deaths and injuries must stop—and simulations training absolutely must continue. It is absolutely essential for our students to win on the street—and they must be taught to win.

They need to know that, if there's a physical struggle, they'll get hit. If they struggle over a knife, they'll get cut. And if they're in a gunfight, they'll get shot. That doesn't mean they'll die from those injuries, but they have to know they can fight through it.

We have recruits fight through a spray of oleoresin capsicum. I've been in a shooting class where my start signal to shoot was a hit from a 50,000-volt stun gun. I've been hit across the knuckle by a Simunitions FX marking projectile from across a room (the guy who shot me wasn't so lucky).

This training, whether we call it simulations or reality-based training or something else, is mission essential. It's important to winning on the street, it's important to making relevant force decisions and to explaining those decisions to those who try to judge those decisions.

Environmental Issues

The training site must be secure and sterile. Officers who enter the site have to know that they cannot bring lethal or active weapons—including knives, guns, ammo, electro-discharge devices, or chemical aerosols—with them. That rule cannot be violated.

If you can get your backup gun into the training site, how do you feel about someone else on the premises pointing a gun at you? Want to stand across the room from another student, watch that student clear his pistol and begin dry practice—using you as a target? Does that make you uncomfortable?

Absolutely no guns in the training area. None. Period.

On the shooting range, even a cold range, I insist on having at least one safety supervisor armed and ready. I'd hate to have someone come into the place and steal our guns! Our sterile role-play area has security on the outside. This outer safety is there to cover incidents that happen close to the training area. We've had someone get a medical retirement because a role-player responded outside to a crime in progress. When the role-player came back in, he forgot to change guns. The trainer caught it and deflected the real gun when it was coming to bear on an officer in training. The fired shot missed but wrecked the trainer's hand.

An outside security supervisor is named as the guardian. The guardian in-briefs trainees. If there's anything the students absolutely have to have inside the training area, they have to get it now. There's no coming back for it. Likewise, they have to check themselves for prohibited items and secure them or surrender them.

The guardian has the officers check their gear and clothing for prohibited items. The buddy system is used. "You've checked yourselves? Who hasn't finished his self-inspection?" If no one speaks up, the guardian instructs them to team up and check each other.

Upon entry into the sterile area, the trainer has the safety officer conduct a thorough safety inspection. This includes checking duty gear, vests—a good place to hide a knife—cargo pockets, coats, and bag baggage. Before going any further, everyone empties his or her pockets. They won't need anything in the scenarios.

The trainer does the final check on each individual or on individual team members before they enter the actual scenario. "Is there anything you shouldn't have that we missed or that you forgot? Please check now."

In this unique environment, they can't "make ready" as they always should. All "nonlethal" devices have to be loaded by a safety coordinator. A student or role-player can watch the loading process. I'd tell them, "At this point, you'd be making ready. Checking your eye protection and your ear protection. Doing a press check and magazine check." Don't actually "chamber check" a Simunitions marking gun. It just pulls the marking projectile loose and you have a mess.

A trainer follows each individual or individual team into the situation. A safe word, already in place, is used to stop action. Don't use "stop," as good officers likely will use that term in a confrontation. One place uses "marshmallow," as it's never been heard during a fight. Find something that works for your training.

Remember to physically check the premises and vehicles used in the scenarios for weapons. When people get excited, they can do a number of things that are unexpected.

While on the subject of physical safety inspections, if any person leaves the training area for any reason, he or she has to stand for another search on return.

Don't slough off on the safety problems inherent with this form of training. One dead officer in training makes for lots of problems besides the obvious.

For example, if there's an accident and an officer is shot in training, how many officers are lost? At least two—the officer who got the bullet and the one who sent it. Add the trainer potentially, as well as the others involved in that training evolution. You might have to add the officers in the agency who never get to receive the training because the administration, horrified by a training fatality, stops it completely.

To Find Out More...

Simunitions Instructor classes are available. Call the Simunition Training Division in Avon, Connecticut, at 1-800-465-8255.

For the information in this chapter, I want to acknowledge the management and staff of the Gunsite Academy, IALEFI, NTOA, XS Sights, Sgt. Jack Morgan (Shawnee County sheriff, retired), Sgt. Chuck Haggard (Topeka [Kansas] Police Department rangemaster), and the trainers who shared their experiences with me.

Join the International Association of Law Enforcement Firearms Instructors (http://www.ialefi.com) and get the Association's Guidelines for Simulation Training Safety, currently costing $25 for nonmembers.

Buy, read, and heed *Training at the Speed of Life*, Vol. 1, by Kenneth R. Murray (Gotha, FL: Armiger Publications, 2004) available at most online booksellers.

Contact Info:

Gunsite Academy, Inc.
2900 W. Gunsite Road
Paulden, AZ 86334-4301
Phone: 928-636-4565
http://www.gunsite.com/home.htm

Simunition Headquarters
5, Montée des Arsenaux
Le Gardeur (Québec)
Canada J5Z 2P4
Phone: 450-581-5999
http://www.simunition.com/index.php

Simunition U.S. Head Office
65 Sandscreen Road
Avon, CT, 06001 USA
Postal Box: P.O. Box 576
Avon, CT 06001-0576
Phone: 860-404-0162

13 The Value of Repetitive Skills Practice

A cop was working a fixed post directing traffic in New York City and was approached by a man dressed in top hat and tails—real formal attire—and carrying a violin case.

"How do I get to Carnegie Hall?" the pedestrian asked the cop.

Without looking at him, the cop replied, "Practice, man. Practice."

It's the same with any motor skills learning. All require extensive repetitive practice, rehearsal, and preparation. Muscles may not have memory, but there is something to neural programming. Go to the ballpark or the stadium, ask any athlete.

"We're going to play for all the marbles now," you tell the assembled team. "No matter what happens or who fouls up, the team that loses is going to be killed or crippled."

They look at each other and then back at you. What?

"Yep, it's hard but that's how life is. This is the big championship. If you lose, you die or get crippled."

"What do the winners get?" a team member asks.

"Well, they live. They get questioned, second-guessed, sued, and prosecuted. And that's nothing—the team lawyer works for the team, not for the individual players. The team can settle, but you have to pay. And the feds can get you and put you away for life."

How many of our youth would leave college early for a chance to play that way?

That's exactly what our cops are playing for—every day they live. If they win, they can lose everything—job, family, freedom, their home—and potentially they can be put to death even if they win the fight. If they lose, it's worse.

Go back to our sports team, or what's left of them. You think those guys are going to play for blood if they don't train and practice? They wreck their joints and their health for a measly few million bucks.

"Our cops aren't athletes," you might reply. Without examining whether cops should be athletes, let's look at our musician. Here's someone who wants a life doing music. Think he'll try Carnegie Hall without preparation?

Then why are our people so unwilling to train? Why do our administrators loathe "losing officers to training." What are they lost *from*?

Managing Training

Argument: "They learned how to shoot in the academy."

Really? Maybe some did and maybe that's the best they ever shot in their careers. It was because someone made them do it and gave them lots of time and ammo to learn to do it. Does that skill stay with you for any length of time?

Let an officer back his car into a light pole in a parking lot and the department just has to have driver training. Again, really? Chances are, that cop drove to work that day. And the day before and the day before that. In fact, that same cop who had that avoidable accident has probably been driving two to nine hours per day for the past several years. Does anyone really think he forgot how? Agencies rack up millions of miles in a single year and managers think driver training stops accidents. Not likely.

But when one cop gets killed in a car stop gone bad, how many people scream for more training on how to fight? I don't hear many voices. Our cop with the accident didn't back into a pole because he forgot how to drive, he got careless. The cop killed on the car stop could well have bought the farm for the same reason. Driver training doesn't teach officers how to drive—it brings their attention to the issue of having wrecks. That *does* prevent accidents. With shooting, it's a different issue. "Oh, it's like riding a bike! You never forget how!"

I can't begin to count the number of times I've seen shooters come to the range and act as if they've never touched a firearm before. I attribute that to a lack of use and contact with the firearm. They simply do the least handling of the gun that they can, to avoid accidents or something. That predictably leads to accidents when, forced by circumstance, they have to try to use it.

You have to be successful in not hitting anything or anyone when you drive a car. It's remarkable, really, how few accidents there are. With a gun on the range, if the cop hits a huge silhouette 30 times or so out of 50—with some rounds hitting the ground in front of the target or splitting target frames—the cop "passes." Is that going to work on the street?

Problem #1: Our Aging Population

Ask any department firearms instructor and he or she will tell you that we have a lot of substandard shooters on the job. For some, it's a matter of the aging process. Our eyes get drier and our corneas stiffen, creating the need for bifocals in people who have gone most of their lives without glasses. In that same group, aging has caused incipient (if not full-blown) arthritis. Repetitive stress generates carpal tunnel syndrome, a nagging problem that hampers trigger control.

Along with aging, many of us fall victim to an occupational fatigue known as burnout. Folks who have done this job for years become resistant to change; their comfort zones become narrow and they fear trying new things—like trying to qualify with new guns or on varying courses of fire.

They've forgotten what it was like to try to make qualification time limits with revolvers. In those days, we were all invincible. Now, we seem vulnerable to a range of diseases, syndromes, and other manifestations of aging. When we focus on our vulnerabilities, we prepare ourselves for the possibility of failure.

Problem #2: Our Rookies

Now, more than at any time in recent history, we are taking on more newly hired cops with little or no relevant marksmanship experience. When we were an agrarian society, we hired many folks with rural backgrounds; farm people tend to know and respect firearms and they tend to have some experience with shooting. Newly hired cops today don't have that sort of history with firearms. Although that may change with the unpleasantness in the Middle East, most military types are forced to run around with unloaded guns! The military is still burdened with the misconception that an unloaded gun is "safe." Nothing could be further from the truth but they are unlikely to listen to reason. That still leaves us with relatively inexperienced gun handlers.

Our population is now largely an urban-suburban one, with few places to shoot, few training opportunities for civilian shooters, and negative press about firearms ownership and usage. We no longer have a significant military draft. Folks with military experience are not always "A" Class shooters but they sometimes know the "little things," like keeping their fingers out of the trigger guard and keeping muzzles downrange.

The lion's share of our new hires are untrained, unprepared, and largely unsafe until they receive some training. Of course, the new hires get the advantage of all that range time at the academy. But after that, how often do they get to a firing range? Or to the Firearm Training System (FATS) simulator? The more years they're with us, the older they get. As they age, we can refer to the aging problem, above.

Worse than all the foregoing, both groups tend to contract "civil service disease." This can be characterized by the oft-heard statement, "If I get no more pay for a higher score, why try harder?"

Problem #3: Boundary Conditions

The borders of our law enforcement community are awash with criticism and hostility from several unrelated and uncoordinated elements.

Use-of-force litigation seems to be at an all-time high. The argument often heard is that because lesser force options are most often used, we should therefore train more intensively in lesser force than in deadly force.

Check the jury awards for the torts of assault and battery and compare them to those in wrongful death actions. Wrongful death properly has a much higher price tag. While training in all levels of force is essential, downplaying deadly force will not serve you well.

Our occupation has been under attack from those who are best served by doing so: plaintiffs' bar, politicians (street-corner and inside the Beltway), and criminals of various types. When we observe a noted law professor and appeals attorney telling the public, on national television, that cops are trained to "testi-lie" in the academies, you have to have grave concerns. Such statements will doubtlessly show up in opening and closing arguments during your officer-student's trial.

As if the litigators weren't bad enough, it seems that street gangs are increasingly ready to take on the police in gun battles, according to Calibre Press, a clearinghouse for officer survival information. Apparently, a number of youths choose to withstand an initiation ritual that includes attempting to murder a cop.

Political extremists, on both sides of the political spectrum, hold an intensive dislike for police authority. Although the right-wing elements are currently getting the most media attention, radicals on the left are no less a threat now than in previous decades. Add to this mess the increasingly dangerous domestic terror cases and the advent of Islamic terrorism, and it seems that gunfighting skills are needed now more than ever.

Goals and Objectives

The law enforcement executive, under his or her judgment and authority, allows the agency's officers to carry guns, in public, understanding full well that an officer may have to shoot in areas where the only backstop is bystanders—taxpaying constituents who only want us to keep them safe. The potential for tragedy is huge. Even though we are more likely to use less-than-lethal force (and that requires training too), few techniques can result in the huge judgments typical for wrongful death actions involving firearms. Low-force encounters usually result in smaller damages compared to the rare shooting that has predictably grave results. Obviously, we need to train across force levels, but we need to continue to emphasize those uses of force with the highest gravity.

The aims of any firearms program are to:

1. Ensure that officers can carry and manipulate firearms safely, even in public.
2. Ensure officers can effectively use firearms (with accuracy, speed, and confidence) to protect themselves and others from deadly threats.
3. Minimize the chances for accidents, unintentional discharges, mistakes, and errors in judgment regarding the use of firearms.

Marksmanship and gun handling are motor skills that require frequent refresher training. Our SWAT team, recognizing the need to sharpen and refresh those skills used most frequently, trained monthly. The Canine (K9) Unit, knowing that their dogs and handlers require regular practice, trained monthly. Are rank-and-file officers less likely to need firearms skills than specialized units? Are they any more likely than police dogs to "just remember" what they need to do?

Our goals and objectives, listed above as the aims of firearms programs, require regular, repetitive practice. We need to train regularly, not in a once-a-year in-service mode.

Skills Maintenance

At the 1996 ASLET seminar, Clive Shepherd of NRA characterized marksmanship as a degradable skill; that's perfectly apparent to firearms instructors nationwide. It's not just marksmanship we are concerned with, however. Gun-handling skills must be honed regularly as well.

The rate of negligent discharges went up greatly as the "police semiautomatic pistol revolution" peaked in the early 1990s. This points to the truth of the argument that regular practice is essential to ensure our own safety from ourselves.

Traditionally, we go to the range to qualify periodically. Some agencies go annually. Others are twice a year, including the New York City Police Department, unless something happens: "Only one qualification cycle was conducted during 2004 with 25,783 uniform members of the service attending the 9mm Qualification Cycle and 1,626 attending the Revolver Qualification Cycle" (http://www.nyc.gov/html/nypd/html/police_academy/police_academy.shtml). The Drug Enforcement Administration (DEA) reportedly qualifies four times a year, as my agency did for some years.

Four times a year. From that, we are expected to carry firearms and safely use them in public, during incidents that are "uncertain and rapidly evolving," most often in reduced light, when there are bystanders nearby. There are often multiple suspects, suspects who shoot at you or attack with an edged weapon, and who move dynamically. Four times a year may not be enough.

Qualification is not an appropriate goal. If you "train to qualify," your training is strictly backwards in its approach. Appropriate goals are officer and constituent safety. We have found abysmal failure rates in qualifications even after massive in-service firearms training. Your department has a legal and moral obligation to train employees for the job they're being asked to do. Marksmanship is an essential primary skill, but it is only one element of a total firearms skills package. Since there are court cases mandating practical training in spite of low budgets, we need to move in the direction of training for the job, verifying the effectiveness of our training via proficiency testing.

Besides, qualification is not training. It's a test, a documentable standard of achievement. Can you safely load and holster the issued handgun? Can you safely draw it and fire it accurately? Can you quickly reload and resume shooting it? Can you unload it, make it safe, and safely maintain it to factory specifications? Are you able to coordinate a flashlight with the gun to effectively fight in night conditions? We seek to answer all these questions and more during qualifications.

What Is Training?

Training is repetitive skill building. Training is using acquired skills in various scenarios, under varying conditions, while demonstrating good judgment in decision making.

If an agency has a gunfight simulator such as FATS, it shouldn't be difficult to get a monthly firearms training schedule off the ground. Most agencies can't afford such a luxury; for them, it's a little more difficult—but not impossible.

Since *Popow v. Margate*, firearms instructors have known that lawsuits for failure to train are hazardous to taxpayers who are obligated to pay high judgments. In attempting to identify where the greatest agency exposures are, current information from NRA was used. The following areas are the most commonly encountered training deficiencies:

1. Teaching officers to think with a gun in their hands
2. Safe movement with firearms in hand
3. Use of cover
4. Reactive targets (the officer shoots until the threat is gone)
5. Moving targets
6. Gunfight simulations
7. De-escalation drills: that is, reducing from deadly force to a lesser force option
8. Extensive gun handling
9. Many agencies only certify with shotgun—they fail to train with it
10. Training trainers

11. No practice
12. No stressors—many agencies have only recently returned to timing qualifications
13. Decision making and problem solving
14. No dim-light training for day-shift personnel and no training in use of flashlight to identify targets
15. No bystanders (no-shoot targets) cluttering up the range
16. No off-duty, plainclothes officer or backup gun training; no training on "authorized weapons"

This list was compiled based on the officers' needs. Officers wander about the community armed—in schools, the courthouse, shopping malls, hospitals, the projects, and rural areas. While the potential for liability is enormous, the cost to prepare our people for these challenges need not be. It's a matter of training smart and being willing to take information from other agencies.

The obvious argument against monthly firearms training is cost. While the roll-call training model has been the cheapest route of regular in-service over the years, roll-call training is far too short for meaningful training exercises of the types we are referring to. As the concept of monthly training was invoked, it was noted that we have SWAT and K9 training monthly. But these specialized units train for an entire day each month. In most agencies, the entire department can't take off that long.

Monthly firearms training, properly planned, can be accomplished in about two hours per officer. Since officers won't be trained individually—small groups tend to train the best—department size shouldn't present a problem. For an agency of about 100 officers, we can schedule to have 5 to 10 officers train at a time. Trainees can arrive, be briefed, execute the training plan, clean up, and leave in a short time.

The key, in training as in survival, is in planning.

Costs and Benefits

Organize training plans that call for low round expenditures. Simply coming out to the range and dumping 50 rounds of ammo in two hours is nearly pointless. We have to use this monthly training as the practice that officers would not do on their own. Repetitive practice is good for all of us: It reinforces the basic training the young officers have recently had, it refreshes the older troops, and it helps us to find ways to accommodate our accumulating disabilities. Monthly training helps prepare us for the emergencies that usually end up agitating folks who look at law enforcement from the outside; it proves that we are making vital attempts to prepare public servants for the proper use of the ultimate force option.

It's intensively relevant to have officers load a first magazine with one round and their other two with two rounds each. Have them practice the speed reload dry first, and then have them load as above. On the command, they will fire one round, instantly reload, and fire a second round. Unless you have turning targets, have them cover the target until they are ordered to "recover." They can reduce to the ready position or reholster, as you like. Have them continue, reloading discarded magazines with two rounds and replacing them in the pouch (snapped in) between stages. In this way, practice in the vital skill of quickly reloading a depleted pistol can be done cheaply and quickly.

Drawing and firing single, accurate shots is another worthy skill to develop. Have them come out one month and do some precision shooting at 50 yards if your range is capable of that distance. Use dummy rounds and make them practice stoppage drills. This could keep them from freezing up when they experience a failure in the field. Practice weapon retention skills.

Frequently switch off between pure marksmanship, gun-handling skills, and tactical exercises that combine all of those skills along with judgment in role-play scenarios. During our 1994 in-service training, we had our officers do a drill inspired by a Massad Ayoob video tape. We had four officers per line, each faced by one target. Each officer had a role-playing colleague next to him or her on the firing line. We advised each officer that he or she was responding to a suspicious circumstance call in which a stranger (the target to the shooter's front) was in someone's backyard in the middle of the night. When the officer challenged the subject, the subject turned and the officer noticed a gun in his waistband. This should cause the shooting officer to draw and cover his or her target. At that point, the role-player took over and spoke on behalf of his or her shooter's target. As the questions and answers shuttled back and forth, it soon became apparent to the officers that they were handling a suicide in progress.

We kept most of them at gunpoint, making attempts at crisis intervention, for 10 to 15 minutes. During this time, they had to talk, listen, and learn how to deal with cramps in their hands and arms. Role-players did their best to irritate their counterparts, often not realizing that the roles would soon be reversed.

All participants wore safety glasses and hearing protection. At the whistle, they were to respond as if the suicidal subject had gone for the gun. They had a second to get two five-zone hits on their targets. This is one drill that has low round usage, and involves judgment and relevant gun-handling skills. There are many others.

To take each of the "Failures to Train" cited above, we proposed the following stopgap solutions:

1. Teach officers to think with gun in hand. We put "faces" and donated clothing on the targets. If we incorporate even a partial turning target system, we force the officers to use judgment in the shooting decision. We can change the structure of some range training to force the officer to act without coaching from range staff.
2. Teach movement with firearms in hand. New training courses—monthly, if possible—should include tactical movement. We can even go back to simulations training periodically to remedy some of these failures.
3. Teach the use of cover. This can be done in regular training by "cluttering up the range" with props and by judicious, periodic simulations training.
4. Use reactive targets (shoot until the threat is gone). Obviously, the best solution is to convert your existing range to a turning target system, if you don't already have one. In this way, every time an officer shoots on the range, the signal to fire will be a target facing the officer. Put photocopied graphics of guns on each target to ensure that the officers only fire when faced with an "armed" target. The officers will be instructed to shoot until the target is neutralized (faces away). Turning target systems are not cheap and homemade ones tend to be troublesome to maintain. Manufactured units are expensive, but well worth the cost. An investment in knock-down steel "Pepper-Popper" targets costs little. They last nearly forever (if properly used and maintained) and, if you hold back some of the department's old body armor, you can wrap the targets in kevlar, cover them in donated shirts, and put photocopied faces from magazine advertisements on the head box. The officers can shoot, close up, at a realistic target.
5. Use moving targets. Our old gravity-fed mover was shot to pieces. If you can arrange the time and get help from some of your department's "construction" people, an electric mover is possible to make at low cost using garage door openers for the motive force. It would be helpful to string one that will run toward the officer and away from the officer to test contact weapon defense skills and their understanding of *Garner v. Tennessee.*
6. Create gunfight simulations. With donated materials and some time from your "construction" people, you could construct a tire house for gunfight simulations. Any officers you employ who have been involved in practical pistol competitions doubtless have some interesting, low-cost ideas for suddenly appearing targets to put in such a structure. Training in this simulator would be especially interesting for your SWAT team as well. If your SWAT team has Simunitions to use in their training, ask them for help; these and frangible rounds are ideal in a tire-house gunfight simulator. Before constructing a shoothouse, do some research. There are safety hazards, including fire issues, that must be addressed.

7. Practice de-escalation drills. To be incorporated in monthly training, officers would be told that the target has ceased lethal attack but is still resisting. The officers have to safely reholster and draw a PR-24 or collapsible baton to deal with the continuing, less-than-lethal threat.
8. Have extensive gun handling. This would be exercised during your monthly training efforts. If nothing else, practice your basic standards as a line drill.
9. Certify with shotgun—and train with it. A low-cost method of training includes the use of cheap birdshot and the use of the metal targets you may already have. Ensure that your people are using impact-resistant eye protection when using any metal targets.
10. Train the trainers. Already discussed above, you can also ask your trainers to contact trainers from other agencies to get input on their training. Further, in the same sense that your specialized units train regularly, your firearms staff should train in house before each firearms training session. In this way, they can hone their marksmanship and teaching skills.
11. Practice regularly. Monthly required training would quiet those officers who complain that the range is never open for practice while ensuring that the range is being properly used. All monthly training and qualifications should be done on an appointment basis. That is, each officer will be scheduled for training and qualification. Personalizing the service in this manner can help in working with "problem shooters" and in allowing for officers absent on leave time.
12. Include stressors. When officers are more confident of their skills, you can add stress by changing targets and using scenarios to test those skills. Trade targets with other departments, making your officers shoot on different targets during each training session.
13. Include decision-making and problem-solving skills. Use scenarios, moving targets, or gunfight simulations in the tire house and with paintballs to increase officers' skills in these areas.
14. Include dim-light training for day-shift personnel and training in use of flashlight to identify targets. This is problematic due to overtime, changing schedules, and keeping neighbors living near the range awake at night. Having people qualify during the shift they work is good, but even day-shift officers have to go into dark buildings or come to work while it is still dark. Some work off-duty security in uniform, at night. One possible, low-cost solution is to ask other nearby agencies for a yearly use of their indoor range to qualify. Require each officer to bring a functional flashlight and turn the lights down.
15. Add "bystanders" cluttering up the range. Add no-shoot targets and items of cover to obstruct view of the targets. Have the moving target move about behind cover.

16. Include off-duty, plainclothes officer or backup gun training, as well as training on "authorized weapons." These issues can each be addressed during regular, periodic training sessions. Officers can be notified that they should bring "authorized" (off-duty or backup gun) weapons and ammunition. Those who only have the issued weapon can solve the problem with the issued gun. Those who have other guns can be called upon to use them in the same situations.

Getting Started

If you can get funding and scheduling approved, one of the best sources for ideas is the Law Enforcement Activities Division of NRA. The Law Enforcement Activities Division is not a political arm of NRA; their concern is safely training officers to save lives in the field.

They offer a Tactical Firearms Instructor Development School around the country every year. The class is concerned with finding low-cost ways to offer the finest in training available. It's not a basic shooting school. There is a marksmanship requirement from the start of the class. This tactical school goes beyond conventional instructors' schools, like tactical training goes beyond simple marksmanship. In today's lawsuit-crazy environment, it is essential training.

The more training opportunities we take throughout the year, the more likely the training will hold between qualifications (skills tests) and between lethal encounters on the street. In this fashion, each officer on the department will have monthly practice in those skills essential for officer safety.

14 The Weapon

Guns are tools. In the same way a hammer and saw are tools for carpenters, the sidearm is a tool of our trade. There's never been a house built by hammer and saw; there have been many built by carpenters armed with hammer and saw.

The fact that a peace officer wears a gun doesn't mean that he or she is armed. In the words of the Chairman (a name given to maestro Jeff Cooper), having a gun makes you no more a gunman than having a Stradivarius makes you a musician.

But what does make one competent?

The Fighting Mind

The Chairman went on to note, "The weapon is not what's between your hands, it's what's between the ears." Nothing is more true. We've seen the incompetent loaded up with munitions. Conversely, we've seen the same type devoid of defensive weapons. I'm no more a carpenter, even if blessed with possession of a hammer and saw, than I am without them. My mind doesn't work that way.

Jeff Cooper came up with a Mindset program that was inspired. While giving the subject complete coverage, his plan was wonderfully simple. I've seen recordings of a few of his Mindset lectures—Wednesday afternoon's class, if I'm not mistaken, at the American Pistol Institute. I've used one video lecture of his in front of classes of recruits and in-service peace officers. I've paraphrased it in classes for criminal justice majors in university. I had no complaints from either. I have seen the language of Mindset adopted by those who didn't go armed. That's fine. It's not about the gun or the condition of readiness of a firearm. It's all about the readiness of the individual.

Cooper worked on "finding what worked" starting over 40 years ago. He organized open competitive matches. There were few limits on what gun could be used, what holsters, how the gun was set up, and, more importantly, how the gun was used to solve the problems he posed. He came to some of the answer that way.

In the first full week of June 2006, I was at the Gunsite Academy. Cooper's home, the Sconce, is on the premises. At the conclusion, Jeff's lovely wife,

Janelle, invited the class members to come over to meet Jeff. I'd spoken to him before at the annual Shooting, Hunting, and Outdoor Trades Show (SHOT).

Jeff was much diminished physically. He had to remain seated for the most part. We were alerted that there should be no mushy accolades but that he was interested in engaging conversation. While physically diminished, mentally he was unaffected and still on his game.

Having my few moments with him, I told him I wouldn't take a lot of time from the rest of the class but I had a question. How had he come to the issue of mental preparation for combat? When he was investigating defensive pistolcraft, how did he come to mind-set as a cornerstone?

"I wondered what set people who faced lethal violence and prevailed apart from those who didn't," he said. "I found that people who won gunfights weren't particularly good shots. But they all knew how to *think*. That's how Mindset started."

Back to the Beast

The problem is one of doing it. Going back to an examination of stress-inspired shooting techniques, we saw that the human response to sudden deadly violence was thought to be "fight or flight." That didn't explain the numbers of people who simply "froze," giving us fight, flight, or freeze. Part of the issue is that humans are (ideally) programmed not to intentionally cause deadly or crippling harm to other humans. That's the way it should be. We have moral (religious), ethical (philosophical), and legal rules against such behavior, but those serve to formalize our common understanding. The nonviolence predilection doesn't exist for those social reasons but is underlying and hardwired.

Wiring can "short out" and our repugnance at violence can be manipulated. Look at movies and video games, let alone upbringing, as issues that allow some to overcome—and others begin to enjoy—violence. Drama, a fundamental human entertainment much predating motion pictures and computers, uses displays of suffering and hardship to invoke desire to do harm to transgressors.

Even so, actually doing someone harm is a different animal. I've spoken to people who'd just engaged in their first fight. "It was nothing like I thought it would be" was a common refrain. It's certainly nothing like the movies.

The problem is one of doing it. Can you press the trigger through with your sights on someone's chest? Our students bring their lives' experiences with them. They wouldn't be there if they didn't think they couldn't do it (I hope). Just sitting here, with no mental preparation, we can't do it. We have to overcome that reluctance to put a bullet through a human being.

One should be reluctant to do so. It's important to avoid hurting people. There are citizens out there who do enjoy killing human beings. When we find them, we try to defuse them by life imprisonment or execution. The question Cooper had to face was, "How do we adjust from this appropriate reluctance to a willingness and ability to do so?"

Inspiration

There are a number of stories that go around about how Jeff identified the elements of his Mindset program. One of them is probably right, but I don't know which it is, and I'm not sure it matters. It seemed to me that he was struck by divine inspiration. More likely, he'd examined the thing at length and allowed it to ferment. I imagine he saw or heard something later that drew him back to the problem. Having made the link, I'm guessing he quickly came to what we now have.

Cooper's Mindset is complete as he laid it out. It requires no more elements or conditions, no additions. Fewer conditions don't cover the subject; more tend to "make it busy," in Jeff's words. Ever concerned with expressing the problem and its solution in a way that people would grasp quickly, retain for a long time, and be able to use reflexively, he labeled his categories as colors, not letters or numbers.

We can't walk around in a prickly posture, "on the prod" and ready to shoot at a moment's notice. It's not appropriate socially and legally. Besides, it's hard on the "machinery." A good friend of a friend died young this way. He'd been raised, lived, and worked in a rough part of Philadelphia. He was always ready for battle and the bad guys never got him. His highly enervated state led to an aneurism, taking him from us early. But we can't sleepwalk either. We have to adjust our awareness level up and down to match existing conditions. And we have to adjust quickly.

White

The first level is the absence of Mindset, what could be called "absence of mind." Many of us engage in this level routinely, though its best use is when asleep. We've all seen people in public who lack attention to their surroundings. They look at the ground as they walk, shoulders hunched, heads down. They drive and can't recall the trip itself—they just know they got to work or home. They'll sit at a red light, talking away in imaginary conversation with spouse or the boss—with no evidence of a cell antenna on their car.

Cooper described this condition as White, like snow blindness. In White, you are unaware, unprepared, and unready. Anyone can take you—unless his incompetence prevents a successful attack—and you cannot respond in time to deal with the threat.

Denial typifies this condition, which is actually more of a state like semi-somnambulism; the way to describe it is, "This can't be happening to me! I want to change the channel!"

Shortly after we'd moved from a smaller town to a big city, my wife and I went to a department store to shop. As married couples tend to do, she went to look at what she wanted to see and I wandered off to look at things that might interest me. I took a look around and, having no money anyway, went looking for her. I found her looking at something on a shelf. I was going to sneak up to startle her, but I realized someone else was watching her.

At that time, the city in which we lived was the home of several mental hospitals. We'd often see some poor soul or another wandering the streets after being released. The guy watching her was likely no threat, but he could have been. He was dressed in an old and tattered field jacket. He was unkempt. Since there was no obvious immediate threat, I thought I'd just wait to see what happened.

Finished looking at the trinket, she wandered off down the aisle and turned left. Watching, I saw her shadow follow down the aisle and turn left. I simply followed along to watch.

For 10 or so minutes, I followed our subject who was following my wife. Eventually, I tired of the game. I walked past our poor soul and up to my wife. In a loud voice, I asked who her friend was and pointed after him.

Having been found out, he quickly moved on and she demanded to know what was going on. I told her, which was an unwise course of action on my part. She was simply in White.

Jeff mentioned that he was reminded of an article (he didn't cite which one) he'd seen in *Scientific American* about a researcher who interviewed strong-arm muggers in a prison. He had interviewed them individually and shown them pictures of street scenes. The question was, who of these people would you try and who wouldn't you try? They agreed with each other 100% of the time: I'd try this one, but I wouldn't try that one. What were they seeing?

They saw the unconnected, unengaged, and self-absorbed as easy targets. They saw people who walked with purpose, head up, looking at everyone around as potential problems. Experienced in the victim selection process, they'd take someone in White, but wouldn't try someone who was alert.

Someone in White can't fight. They tend to react hysterically, they may try to run away, they often freeze. Attempts to comply with violent criminals are less successful in this era. They tend to kill anyway, even if the victim is compliant. We shouldn't be in White at any time we're around people we don't know. In any public venue, while driving, or walking for exercise, we need to move out of White. When we move away from White, we move into a balanced level of preparation, Yellow.

Yellow

Yellow is a description of relaxed alert. The officer or citizen is simply aware of surroundings and other people in the area. When driving into the parking lot of a convenience store, being in Yellow, we look to see what's happening inside. We examine people in the lot. We don't just get out and wander in, counting money.

Someone in Yellow may drive by once and give the place a look. People in Yellow tend to use drive-up windows and pay at the pump for fuel. Look at everyone around you.

Condition Yellow is no more than a realization that the world is an unfriendly place. It's the statement, spoken to oneself when making ready at the start of one's day, "I may have to use the cartridge in the chamber of this pistol to shoot someone today."

Yellow is distinct from other levels in that it is nonspecific. You have no target or potential target. You are simply looking around, actually seeing what happens around you. It can actually be likened to "smelling the roses." You will see things you've never seen before—or, more precisely, things you may have seen that you failed to take note of.

Jeff would say that someone in Yellow was like a patrol craft on the surface of the ocean, radar antenna rotating 360 degrees all the time. You don't want trouble and you aren't seeking trouble, but you are looking out for it. If that radar gets a "blip," you move up a level.

Orange

Orange is differentiated from Yellow by being specific. It's not "I may have to shoot someone today;" it's "I may have to shoot *him* today." Your "radar" found a target, or a potential target, worthy of your lethal attention. If he has attracted your attention, he has to be examined until you determine he's not a problem.

That doesn't mean that the radar sweep stops; that's the basic decoy situation. Someone attracts your attention while someone else attacks from 6 o'clock. You have to keep attention on the problem while maintaining your 360-degree sweep. Not easy? No, it's unsettling as it can be. Just don't concentrate on the subject to the exclusion of the rest of the world.

Condition Orange is not a threat to the person who's come to your attention. He's in no danger. You've simply adjusted your mind to the likelihood that you may have to use force on this person sooner rather than later.

When wandering about in the department store described earlier, I was in Yellow. When I went in search of my wife and found a man following her around, I moved up a notch to Orange. "I may have to use some level of force against this guy. Watch him!" When he retreated after I'd called him to her attention, I dropped back to Yellow. Simple.

What if he had, in Jeff's words, hoisted the Jolly Roger and declared himself? In that case, we move to Red.

Red

Red means fight. This doesn't mean that there is shooting or grappling or handcuffs—yet. It means that the decision has been made. This person is a threat and I'm taking no chances.

In Red, you set your mental trigger. "If he does this thing…," draws a gun, turns toward me, whatever the situation calls for, "I'm using force and stopping the threat." There is no longer any need for mental discussion or debate. The issue of "Is he a threat?" has been addressed and we've concluded we're going to war. The only thing we're waiting for is for him to trip our mental trigger.

I responded to a call to receive information about a "past violent domestic" in which "the male half isn't present." The victim/complainant was at a convenience store during its rush hour. My back unit was 20 or so minutes behind me. The scene I witnessed as I rolled up made the hair stand up on my neck. A nicely dressed woman was near the door of the store. The look on her face was one of hysterical panic and desperation. She was looking at a man standing in the lot.

Customers walked past this tableau oblivious to the scenario. This was going to get messy. A stampede would likely result when the guns went off. I was still driving up when I got on the radio. I simply said that the male half had arrived and to have my back "step on it." Before I dismounted, I shut off my portable radio, for reasons that will become apparent soon.

I saw a man with the blankest stare I'd ever seen, to that point in my life. He stared through me and into my soul. It felt like he was looking at the place he needed to hold to ensure his gunfire reached my heart.

The woman started to approach me. I told her to get in the building, get the door locked, and call 911. I didn't even look at her, but I heard the door shut, voices raised, as the door was locked.

I walked laterally toward the door, putting myself between the store and the well-dressed man with the "thousand-yard stare." As he stared through me, I moved laterally until a gas pump was between us. He moved out a little to see me and I sidestepped again.

I don't remember hearing the straining engines of the vehicles belonging to a fish and game agent, a motor carrier inspector, and a highway patrol trooper. I do recall seeing them run in my direction. I pointed at the man and said, "If he moves, shoot him." Suddenly the thousand-yard stare gave way to panic as cops totaling something between 300 and 400 pounds piled upon him. Happy they arrived, I went to receive the details of the case. Apparently, the day before, the victim had a pistol pointed into her face by the gentleman outside the convenience store. His countenance and her panicked look had given me the relevant information before she spoke a word.

In a sudden and meteoric rise, I'd gone from Yellow, past Orange, and into Red, where I stayed until the offender was stuffed into the pavement. I'd never drawn my pistol. I had already decided, as I ordered the victim into the store, that if the man moved his hands and arms in a manner similar to the drawing of a gun, I was going to try to put nine rounds of .45 auto into him before he hit the ground. I think he understood that and was trying to build up the nerve to get me to shoot him. We later found out that he had real problems with depression and it was likely he was after a "suicide by cop." He nearly made it.

That wasn't a time to be listening to or trying to talk on a police radio. There was nothing between me and an apparently armed offender but air. Air doesn't stop bullets soon enough to suit me, so the radio was off. I'd set my mental trigger and was waiting for him to trip it when the cavalry arrived. I'm glad they did.

In Red, the decision to fire or fight in other ways has been made. Whether or not that happens is up to your opponent. He decides whether or not there will be a fight. He is responsible for his own fate.

As you move up along the levels of the color code, your unwillingness to use violence and press the trigger decreases. You almost can't pull the trigger in White. In fact, the fight is often over before you knew there was one. In Red, the decision has already been made and you've accepted the likelihood.

Likewise, it's easy to reduce the condition level. If you determine that the individual with the unsightly lump under his jacket is an air marshal, then reduce the condition of readiness from Orange to Yellow.

Stress Loading

How stressful is it to maintain this watchful lifestyle? That depends on your environment and how perceptive you are. Basically, Yellow is known as relaxed alert. As long as you're not asleep, you can stay in Yellow as long as you live. It's not hard. It's a matter of accepting that you may have to use force and violence before this day is over. You may have to shoot for your life.

In fact, you often see a potential problem before that problem notices you. You also find that you put off a neurolinguistic warning flag to all would-be predators—"Pick someone else."

Orange is tough. Since you have a specific potential target and you have to resolve that situation without losing your general, nonspecific alert, it's hard on the nerves. You may have to watch him longer than you want, but watch him you must.

In Red, you have a fight or an incipient fight. Fights are usually over pretty quickly.

There's your chart—White, Yellow, Orange, Red. Some institutions have added a fifth condition, Black, meaning the war is on. In that stage, we're too busy fighting to be worrying about it, so we use the Mindset program as it was brought down from the Mount.

As you go through life, adjust your mind-set to the environment. Whenever you leave your home, move to Yellow. Stay in Yellow until you get a potential threat or you are safely back home.

When on the job, it's an occupational requirement to be in Yellow. A car stop calls for an immediate move to Orange—you don't know who is in that car, do you? It surprises people how easily and transparently the color code works as you practice it. When watching film or television, ask yourself what condition that character was in...and what condition he should have been in.

The Best Gun (and Gear) 15

Which One Is Best?

Firearms instructors find themselves in the position to answer this question more than anyone else in the outfit. There are some members of the service who think they know better than we; perhaps they do. But the chief, sheriff, or director is knocking on your door. The peace officer is often asked, with a pointed finger at the holstered sidearm, "Is that a *forty-five*?"

They try not to sigh. It's about as common as Uncle Fred seeing you arrive at the family Christmas party with the comment, "Uh-oh! The law is here! They're after you!" or "You won't like it here, we have no doughnuts."

What is the best gun for your officers? What is the best holster, the best load? There are a few answers, and one, I promise, will leave you unhappy.

The Best?

I thought I was the first to answer this way, but I'm misinformed. I find that a large number of instructors got to the answer long before I did.

The best gun in the world is *the one that's in your hand* when the fight starts! You might wish it were a 1911 or a Magnum revolver, a bigger caliber or smaller, but we have to go with the starting lineup. There is no other real choice. It's that or give up.

At one point in my checkered career, I carried a 4-inch .357 Magnum because that's what was issued. It was loaded with ammo that I didn't prefer. The ammo wasn't unsafe but it wasn't my choice. I carried it and kept my counsel close. When we got .45 autos in 1986, I still didn't get to comment on ammo selection. We were issued really good ammo that had an unfortunate name. It lasted only a year and then we went to a known accuracy load. The following two years we got a load with a dynamic bullet design. After that, it was back to a more conventional jacketed hollow point but loaded to higher pressures. That stayed with us for several years, until we bought ammunition from the state bid roster. We eventually bought guns in another caliber.

Figure 15.1 Things have changed a lot over the past 30 years. When I started in law enforcement, guns like this Smith & Wesson Model 66-1—a 4-inch stainless steel .357 Magnum—were carried. Semiautos in police holsters were rare.

The first load issued with our most recent new autos? The ammo that came in a package deal with the guns, what else?

Needs for Your Agency

How do you assess weapon, ammo, and gear needs for your agency? Well it may surprise some, but cost is a factor. If it weren't, maybe we'd all be carrying $3,000 custom 1911 pistols, but I doubt it.

Cost is a huge deal. It makes sense to be concerned about the budget. A few years before this was written, the smart money on long guns was for the AR-15/M-4 style carbine. At that time, magazines were widely available—even for individual purchase in spite of the 1994 gun ban—and ammo was dirt cheap. Trying to find any 5.56 × 45mm ammo that's currently less than $400 per thousand is a real chore. Ammo for the shotguns, while more expensive than in years gone by, is becoming more attractive.

Environment

Where do your officers work? If you work in a densely populated inner city, that may cause a bias in your guns and ammo selection. It may have an impact

Figure 15.2 This officer fires a qualification course in the "old days." The bent knees and forward-tilted shoulders look like what we are preaching today. The more things change, the more they stay the same.

on holster selection too, but the most secure holster that your slowest employee can quickly draw from is what I'd choose for issue—if we had to issue it. I'd rather have an approved list and reimburse the officers for their selections.

If your officers work in the metroplex, I wouldn't use 7.62 × 51mm rifles as patrol rifles. For a state fish and game agency or highway patrol, I might look at the 7.62 for a more general issue. A county agency where there is a larger city (100,000-plus), a large suburban development, some smaller villages, and considerable rural area would likely find use for some 7.62 rifle deployment as well.

That pretty well described the agency I used to serve. They've gone to AR-style .223 carbines, a superb choice as well as being easier to train with. The ammo has gotten pricey, as indicated.

Along with exterior environment, what is the agency environment? How is the department populated? If it's like most departments, there are a number of officers who are of "smaller stature," a term I recognize as euphemistic of "female." We had a number of male officers who were slightly built as well. Larger officers can also have small hands, and hands run firearms.

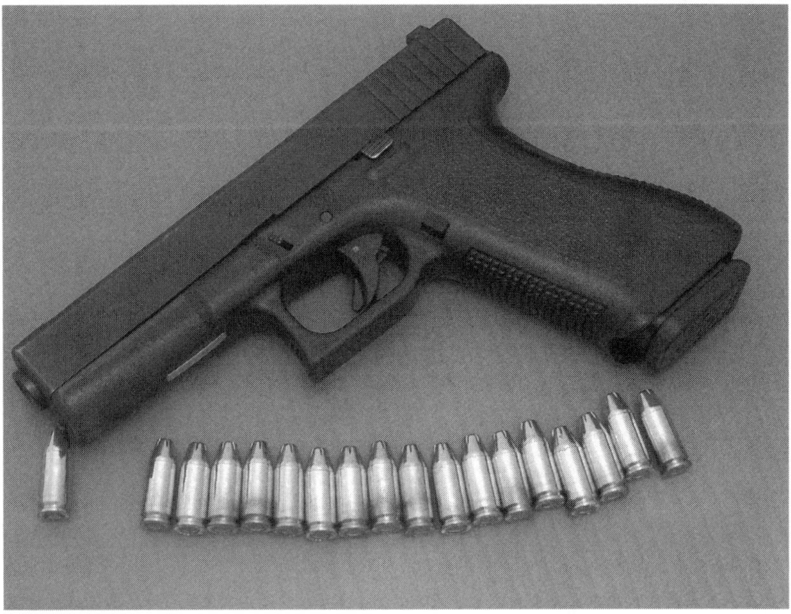

Figure 15.3 The Glock 17 is a service pistol of long standing. Lightweight and reliable, the G17 has a capacity of 17 rounds in the magazine plus one in the chamber.

Early in the morning of the day I penned this chapter, I was having breakfast with a retired sheriff and a retired undersheriff. The sheriff noted that his idea of the ideal gun is a .22 Magnum pistol with a 30-round capacity backed up by a carbine of the same caliber with a 150-round magazine.

How did he get there? He's seen how cops shoot. They miss, operationally, all the time. He's hoping that the miss will hurt less with the smaller cartridge, though he realizes that the .22 Magnum is a nasty little cartridge that can do lots of damage to someone's insides. He figures cops will be more accurate with something that kicks less, has less blast, and has fewer consequences with a miss.

He's almost right. I disagree with the "fewer consequences of a miss" angle, but the rest is dead on. For the biggest part of my career, I've seen a lot of "non-gun people," a number of whom lacked size or strength but more often lacked willingness, who have to shoot guns that were large and powerful. Four-inch .357 Magnums, steel frame .45 autos with 5-inch barrels, and full-power ammo just wasn't going to work for them.

The New York City Police Department did "okay" for many years having non-gun people carrying 4-inch .38 Special revolvers, a number of whom now carry Glock 19 9mm handguns.

Figure 15.4 One factor in the Glocks' favor is that they are available in different sizes: the G17 (right) is the full-size service pistol. The G19 (center) is the compact version, good for the small statured or for detectives, and the G26 subcompact, good for backup status or off-duty. The G17 carries 17+1, the G19 is a 15-shot 9mm, and the G26 carries 10 rounds in the magazine.

Gun People

I'm a gun guy. When I got out of uniform, went to detectives, and was able to make a choice, what did I go to?

I was approaching the last years of my career. Arthritis was catching up. Besides, as a writer for firearms publications, I was getting to shoot a lot of guns—a number of which were more powerful than I wanted or needed. This doesn't help the joints any. Besides, I was getting to practice for the fight less and less often. I usually shot reliability and accuracy tests. So I looked around, considered the weight of the gun against the payload, and looked to see if concealment holsters were actually available.

This is similar to a needs assessment I would do for the outfit a few years later. What gives us (1) reliability, (2) light weight, (3) ease of maintenance, (4) that would fit most shooters, (5) that has a wide selection of duty holsters available, and (6) would be easy to shoot without lots of training?

In my needs assessment, I looked at the cost of the gun and the cost of ammunition in that caliber as well. Like many members of service at NYPD, I selected the Glock 19. It has a payload of 15 in the magazine with another chambered. I carried the gun with a pair of spare 15-round magazines while on duty and off, giving me 46 rounds with which to fight. The Glock 26—a microsize version of the same gun that takes the same magazines—was on my ankle. It had 10 rounds in the magazine with another chambered. That's 57 rounds of ammo with the main gun's magazine able to work in the small gun's magazine well. I felt well served.

I got a certain amount of flack from those who think smaller calibers indicate a small supply of testosterone, but their nonsense fell on deaf ears. The agency subsequently went with Glock, getting the Glock 22 in .40 S&W. This was a department where members carried a .45 auto from 1986 to 2003. It wasn't the time to go from .45 to 9mm for a large number of them. The loadout for a patrol officer with the Glock 22 was the same as for me with a Glock 19: 46 rounds. For some of our deputies who could be waiting for up to 30 minutes for a backup officer, the G22 was a good combination of power and capacity.

It's easily handled. The .45s had a long, trigger-cocking pull for the first shot with a short, light trigger press for subsequent shots. It took a lot of hard practice to be perfect with that mess. The Glock didn't have a world-class match trigger, but the trigger pull was the same for each shot fired. Unlike the bigger (and much heavier) gun, the Glock didn't have a magazine disconnector or thumb safety. If you saw the gun in someone's hand and the finger was on the trigger, you needed to see nothing else—the gun would fire. Some had a bad habit of trigger-checks (putting their finger on the trigger to ensure that the gun was still there) from the .45s. You can get away with that sometimes, if lucky, when you have a 15-pound trigger that sweeps through almost 3/4" of travel before ignition backed up by a manual safety. Don't try it with anything else.

The Armorer's class for Glock is one day, $100, including a paid lunch and you get the armorers' toolkit, which consists of a 3/8" punch. Our previous gun had an armorer's school that was three-to-five days and you had to know how to file a straight line. Holsters were universally available, as Glock pistols held over 70% of the American police market at the time we selected them.

Ammunition

Many will have you believe you need to have a "jello-shoot" put on by an ammo manufacturer to tell you what ammo to carry. That may be, but the rule in 21st-century America is this: Premium hollow-point ammunition made by any respected manufacturer will work most of the time.

"What gets the most one-shot stops?" you'll be asked. There is likely an answer somewhere and it is irrelevant. It doesn't matter how many shootings resulted in a one-hit cessation of hostilities. A number of those incidents are one-hit stops because the shootee "gave up" and just quit fighting.

Figure 15.5 The FNH FNP9 is a high-capacity polymer 9mm that has a traditional double action. The decocking lever is on both sides of the frame. The backstrap can be changed to adjust for larger or smaller hands. It is also available in .40, and a .45 auto is to be released in 2008.

Anecdotal data is "good news, bad news." One offender had his chest shredded by 00 buckshot from a short 12-gauge at fairly close range. His response? To outrun the police until he was going up the stairs of a brownstone. The first officer behind him put a .38 roundnose slug through our Olympian's butt, fracturing his pelvis. He fell backwards down the stairs to the waiting officer. Does this mean the 158-grain roundnose lead bullet from a .38 Special is more powerful than nine pellets of Express 12-gauge buckshot?

Follow that up with an individual who took a number of rounds from a cop's .45 auto but was using cover (i.e., still thinking and fighting) to keep shooting at the cop. While he was thinking, he wasn't thinking hard enough and he kept coming out at the same place to shoot at the officer. The officer, nearing the end of his ammo supply, held on the place where the offender's head came out to shoot. When the offender stuck his head into the open again, a .45 ACP bullet went into his left eye. His lesson? Don't be predictable. The officer's? Use good shooting fundamentals.

It's not the size of the dog in the fight, I've heard it said, it's the size of the fight in the dog. While my gun was only a 9mm, it was loaded with department-issued Winchester 115-grain JHP +P+ law enforcement only

Figure 15.6 The Beretta Px4 Storm is a high-capacity pistol. This example is a C model—"Constant Action." It has a consistent trigger pull shot-to-shot. It's extremely accurate and soft-shooting. It is available in 9mm, .40 S&W, and .45 ACP.

ammunition. Very powerful indeed, the load goes over industry standards to make velocity. It's still more easily handled than a 4-inch .357 Magnum revolver or a .45 auto.

Jim Cirillo had been in 17 personal gunfights and had overseen the results of over 200 more during his time in the NYPD Stakeout Unit. He told me he'd seen people shot with ".38s, 9mm, .45s, .30 Carbine, .223, 12-gauge buckshot, and slugs," among other things. He was still seeking the bullet that guaranteed the one-shot stop up to the day he left us at age 76.

Part of the answer to "what's the best ammo?" is "what can you shoot best?" In my case, it was 9mm, because the biggest identifiable component to this mythical beast called "stopping power" is bullet placement. If you miss, you wasted time and that round was irrelevant—except to the "unintentional target" that received it! If you hit center and he's still fighting, shoot again. And again.

Some people continue to fight because they don't understand that they've sustained an "unsurvivable hit." If you stay out of their deadly grasp and they have time, they will get the message.

Figure 15.7 This SIG-Sauer is the wildly popular P229. This sample has the DAK (double-action Kellerman) trigger—another consistent trigger with no decocker required. The P229 is available in 9mm, .40 S&W, and .357 SIG. The P229 is issued by a number of federal agencies.

Figure 15.8 The compact HK P2000 has three extra backstraps: extra-large, large, and small. The medium is fitted to the gun. Available in 9mm and .40 S&W.

Figure 15.9 When a gun is properly fitted to the shooter, you get good results on target and a smile from the user.

Figure 15.10 The HK P2000 sample had the LEM (Law Enforcement Modification) trigger. This is a consistent trigger with no need to decock before holstering.

Figure 15.11 The gripping surface of the G21SF is more like the G17 9mm, but the G21SF is a .45.

So, 9mm Is Best?

No. Some people I know are best fit with .45 autos just due to their size and mass. Even in my current state of disrepair, I've carried a .45 recently. A Glock 21SF (the "SF" standing for "short frame") came in for testing. This is a 13-shot .45 auto and the gripping surface of the frame has been reduced to the point that it's almost as small around as my favored G19. I put this full-size, relatively high capacity .45 pistol into a Comp-Tac Victory Gear/Minotaur inside-the-waist holster and carried it concealed for a few weeks. That gun has 27 rounds between the main magazine, the spare I carried, and the one in the chamber—with the .45 auto round, that's heavy.

Some of my former colleagues would let me back in the he-man club if only they knew I was carrying that big .45 concealed. Today, I was wearing the full-size Smith & Wesson M&P9. A 17-shot 9mm, I carried it and a spare magazine on my belt along with a 5-shot .38 in a front pocket. I had spare ammo for the .38 as well. Why wear it? The Glock 21SF had gone back in the safe and the 9mm—along with its lower cost ammo—had come out for a pistol class I was taking. I felt quite well armed with either gun.

There are .45s out there now that are more size friendly. The Glock 21SF is just one. The Beretta Px4 is available in .45 ACP, as is the Fabrique Nationale Herstal (FNH) polymer pistol (FNP-45). HK has recently released their HK45. The Smith & Wesson M&P45 is nearly the same size as the M&P9/40.

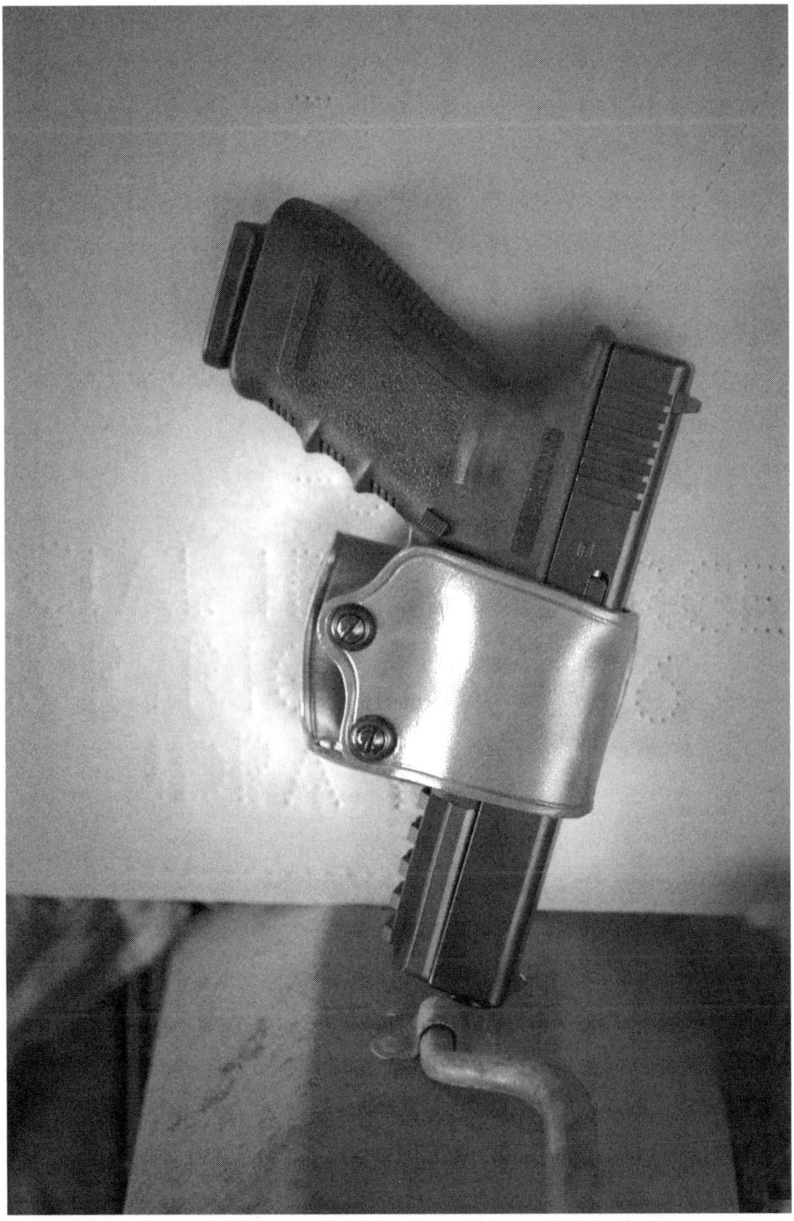

Figure 15.12 The Glock 21SF is a "short frame" (measured from front of the gripping surface to the backstrap). With a magazine capacity of 13 rounds of .45 ACP, it can be carried concealed and still be a decent service pistol. The holster is a Galco Yaqui Slide.

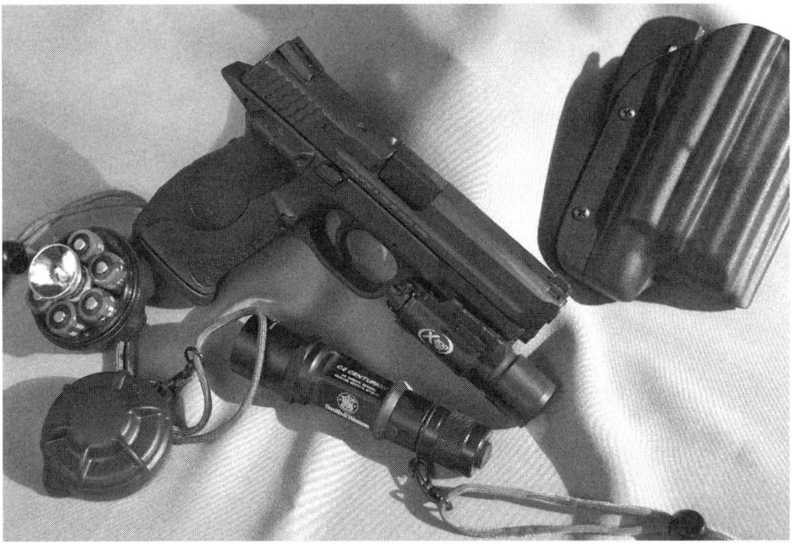

Figure 15.13 This M&P9 is accessorized. The backstrap, which can be changed for size reasons, has been replaced with a Crimson Trace LaserGrip. There is a SureFire X300 gun-mounted light on the accessory rail with a Centurion handheld light and spare battery holder. The holster is by Blade-Tech.

Needs Assessment

The first element of the needs assessment is whether everyone needs to carry the same handgun. I'm aware of the ammo/magazine compatibility argument, which goes as follows: I am engaged and pinned down by superior forces and have run out of ammo. You arrive on scene but can't get me more ammo because you carry a different caliber or, if you have the same caliber but a different make of gun, your magazine won't fit my gun. Therefore, we all have to carry the same gun in the same caliber.

It's rubbish because, if you're close enough to throw ammo or magazines you could (1) solve the problem yourself—if I haven't solved it with my entire load out, what makes you think more ammo will help? Or (2) you could throw me a whole, loaded gun. What, you don't carry a spare gun? Shame on me for poor accuracy and on you for failing to be prepared.

So we don't need the same gun or caliber. Having the same caliber is helpful for supply issues and costs, so I can be persuaded. The gun has to fit the shooter—any of the potential shooters and all of them. Does one gun do that?

No. We're a lot closer with the Beretta Px4, HK P2000, S&W M&P, Walther P99, FNH FNP pistols, the new Ruger SR-9, and the Glock 21SF, but there is no real "one size fits all." Why should there be? We can't all wear the same size uniform. Imagine that uniform bid. "We need three short-sleeve,

Figure 15.14 The SIG-Sauer P220 is a .45 auto. This version also has the DAK trigger. SIG-Sauer pistols are known for accuracy and reliability.

Figure 15.15 HK's new HK45 has all of the currently popular characteristics: it has a slim gripping area on its polymer frame, the backstrap can be changed to accommodate the shooter, and there is an integral accessory rail in the dust cover. This version is not the LEM; it's a traditional double action with a decocking lever and safety on the left side.

Figure 15.16 The S&W M&P9 is a nice-sized service gun. The backstrap is the small version.

Figure 15.17 The Walther P99QA has a consistent trigger pull for every shot. Duty holsters are available and the pistol is quite accurate, as shown here.

Figure 15.18 The M&P is also available in the Compact size. The Compact (top) is shown with the flat magazine floorplate in place.

three long-sleeve, and three trousers each for 200 officers. And they're all the same size." That should limit costs and refitting.

The seats in the patrol cars move closer to the dash as well as further back. This indicates that our officers aren't possessed of the same altitude. Gloves and boots come in different sizes. Guns do too, but we all have to carry the same one.

Again, rubbish. Get the gun that fits the shooters. If you decide on the S&W M&P, get some of the Compact model in your caliber for smaller officers. The M&P9c (Compact) carries 12 rounds of 9mm. There's nothing wrong with that if you can find a duty holster for it.

One agency close by requires "Glock in 9mm." The policy doesn't say which Glock 9mm. It doesn't matter to them. That makes plenty of sense to me.

Figure 15.19 The Smith & Wesson Military and Police pistols are geared toward law enforcement use. Easy to maintain with a short armorers' class, they have proven to be reliable and soft-shooting. The M&P Compact can be used as a service pistol if an appropriate duty holster can be found. The full-size M&P (top) has been carried concealed by the author.

The guns you select must be reliable. That's the single most important requirement: It has to run all the time. These are police guns and are often carried in adverse conditions. They have to work.

The guns shouldn't weigh a lot. Look at all the stuff we're putting on their belts and in their cars. They don't need more junk, they need more training. They're weighed down enough as it is.

Figure 15.20 To enhance handling characteristics of the Compact M&P, one magazine is provided with an extended floorplate.

The armorers' schools must be short in duration, easily found, and cheap. It shouldn't take long to do an annual inspection on the gun. I remember we had guns that required a few hours apiece when a captain did the inspections. When a sergeant took over as armorer, the captain decided that each gun should take 30 minutes for the same annual inspection.

In any event, they need to be easily stripped and cared for. There has to be a wide selection of holsters, uniform, and concealment, for your choice as well.

Finally, the more complex the gun is, the more training time you need to devote to it. If you're unwilling to spend a lot of time in transition and in service, get something easier to use.

We had an agency that had trigger-cocking triggers for the first shot with light pulls for the remaining rounds. The gun was fitted with a "decocker," which dropped the hammer so the gun could be holstered. The rangemaster told me that he spent hours of each biannual in-service day just getting them to decock the pistols prior to holstering. I asked what his success rate was.

"By the end of the day, over 90% would reliably decock the pistol."

I asked about the rate of failures to decock in simulations training. "Oh, it's 100%." Everyone failed to decock after the stress of scenarios!

When I mentioned this to a trainer from another state, he immediately postulated that it was "failure to train." No, it sounds like the topic was covered. Officers didn't believe it was as important as drawing and making hits while not being shot. Why they didn't realize it was important to be able to quickly holster if they had to go "hands on," I don't know.

Figure 15.21 Another size-friendly .45 is the S&W M&P45. Carrying 10 rounds in the magazine, it's a slim, accurate, reliable, and soft-shooting .45.

I used to go along with everyone being above the bar and doing the right thing even if it was hard to get done. I'd like to believe we could still do that, but we can't. We're more interested in community-oriented policing and other socially responsible issues—until the gunfire starts. Then we wonder why our cops aren't competent.

We have it the wrong way around: They need to be able to be cops, to fight, get custody and control, and then be able to recite the need for community policing. The bottom line is that, during a fight, they have enough to worry about without having to horse around with two different trigger pulls and wondering if the gun is cocked or decocked. They need something they can grab, point, and press to get the job done.

It needs to be able to be shot accurately without lots of training because they're not going to get lots of training. And *that's* too damn bad.

The Life

16

Why do people even submit applications to become firearms instructors? Some are gun people and that helps fulfill a part of their lives. Others like to get up and perform—though that number is likely far too few. Some are assigned the job because the boss can trust them; these people may know little of the subject matter and may not present worth a damn, but they will look out for the boss and for the outfit—aspects that are also important.

Others may like to work outside or like to coach people. There may be other reasons, but none of us knew exactly what we were getting into when we entered the life. There were aspects of this thing that I never saw, and issues developed that completely took me by surprise. It wasn't at all what I started out to do and that's fine. It's a rich, full existence. That's not to say that it's a task without tribulations. We all face them and will again.

Those tribulations bind us together. We can be almost as competitive and petty as other types. Each of us believes we have "the answer." That moment is fleeting with the realization that different students require different methods or techniques to get to the place where they can perform without thought—respond reflexively with life-saving skills.

If it sounds like I'm sad, I am a little. It's been a long run with so many things I'd have liked to do left undone. It's the end of my time. I don't know where you are in your run but the issues raised in this book should help you think about your career, should help you form the remainder of it. Agreement with everything presented—or with anything presented—isn't necessary. If what was written here drives you to respond—with a class of your own, with an article in IALEFI's *Firearms Instructor* magazine, or just makes you think about what you do critically—then this book is a success.

I've lost Harland "Bo" Bonner, Dan Rhyne, Jeff Cooper, and Jim Cirillo. In your time, you'll lose mentors, teachers, friends, and colleagues. It's my deepest wish that you lose no students in battle, that we keep the wall of the National Law Enforcement Officers Memorial bare.

This chapter contains my thoughts about the life of a firearms instructor. I'll try to give good advice, maybe something you can use—and some things for which you will hopefully have no need.

The Students

One of the specific requests from the peer reviewers of this project was to deal with the issue of the problem student. What can you do with a recruit who just doesn't get it? How do you reach the poor performers?

Actually, that's the $64,000 question. If I had the answer, I could solve a lot of problems and make a little money. Over the years, I'd change my approach, use different terms to explain the "how"; I'd do various demonstrations and give the student over to other instructors.

Everything I've tried has worked on one or another problem child. Nothing has worked on everyone. Going to another instructor has the advantage of ridding the student of possible issues with the first trainer, and sometimes just another bright, smiling face solves the problem.

Jim Cirillo told of a student he'd had who was not a young recruit but a recruit who was nearing—if not actually well into—middle age. It was apparent she was unfamiliar with firearms except for exposure to TV and movies. Upon shooting for the first time, she put her hand up. Jim approached and she told him, "The gun! It makes noise! It smokes!"

Never one to be able to control his humor, he instantly turned to another range officer and said, "Officer, this recruit's gun makes noise and smokes. Go in and get her one that doesn't."

I've never been able to read trainees the way I could read people on the street. They never failed to amaze me. I've had some who seemed like real hard-chargers who proved themselves to be duds and I've had others make huge efforts to succeed whom I had thought weren't capable. The overwhelming majority fall into the middle, having a moderate amount of skill, desire, and willingness.

A number of officers who were barn-burners when younger congratulate themselves when they hit the backstop now. It's wonderful to see an older officer duck his head, put his hand on his forehead to shade his eyes, see him squint, and hear him say, "Is that a *target* way down there?"

"How can I be expected to hit it from 25 yards if I can't even *see* it?"

Well, for the past 25 years I've told you that your focus should be on the front sight. That thing is only 30-some inches in front of your eyes. About the time one of them responds that I taught him that he shouldn't shoot unless he can visually identify the threat, I'm going to (a) order up an eye exam with a letter to the sheriff and (b) notify state motor vehicle that this particular driver needs a vision test!

I want them all to succeed. I want them all to stay safe and to retire with the same number of holes in their body they had when they started the job. I want them to do their jobs and not be messed over or messed with. So I do my best to take care of my end of the bargain.

Resentment

This section refers to hurt feelings on the range. It may surprise some who've not yet worked as a firearms instructor, but there are people who will get their feelings hurt when you try to help out. Unlike some rangemasters and firearms instructors, I'm easy on people. I know how easy it is to make mistakes. I lost personal control only once and that was when an officer absentmindedly pointed a loaded, cocked DA auto at another person on the line. I almost immediately felt bad about it; there is no excuse for getting excited, but I'd never had anything so stupid happen in my presence. The officer I berated never beefed about it. He didn't go downtown and whine, just sucked it up. Incidentally, I never witnessed him mess up that way again.

The ones who did complain? It was always something silly—to me. It seemed quite important to them. The problem is one of ego. I'm out there to try to get students some relevant training and practice. I have no investment in that except that (1) it must be safe, (2) they have to get something out of it, and (3) I'd like for them to have fun. On the other hand, we seem to periodically get someone with an agenda.

I remember a transition class we did late in my career. We had the poorly named "bullet bucket" outside that we kept loaded with .40 ball ammo. Troops would fill magazines between exercises and it was a way to get a quick turnaround. I'd gone back in the range house and saw one particular male student's notebook lying open. I had time to see "sexual harassment," apparently relative to something I'd said in the classroom component of the training. Our transition to a new firearm was not universally appreciated and I wondered where this would go.

Going back outside, my attention was called to the ammo bucket. Some "unknown person" put a 9mm round in the loose ammo. I can only surmise that this dopey saboteur thought a nine would blow up a .40. I made a production out of it, showing everyone the round and explaining how it was their responsibility to ensure they used appropriate ammo in their guns. We topped off the performance by firing the 9mm out of a company gun. I'm unaware of any nonsense at headquarters after the class, but I think I know who dropped the 9mm into the ammo bucket. I'm still not sure why.

I'd think that, early in the game, we'd learn that ego has no place in this business. Letting people get under your skin causes nothing but trouble on the street, let alone in a training environment. I remember at HK there was a sign over the entrance to the classroom: "Leave your EGO at the door." Presumably you could pick it up again on the way out. That sign needs to be posted at the range, the mat room, and the door leading from roll call to the parking lot.

Tasks

"Man, they got it made," one officer says to another during firearms in-service. "Look at the tan the Sarge has. He comes out here every day, puts on the sunscreen, and yells at us. That's all he has to do."

Really? I bet none of them wondered who built the target frames—or who had to get a truck and drive down to get the lumber for them. They probably believe that housekeeping comes out to keep the range house straightened. And leaving a little of that brass on the ground "for seed" doesn't hurt anyone. You don't see that aging old cop bending over to pick all that up.

Who mows the lawn, shovels the snow, fixes the building alarm—and fixes the gate about the 15th time a drunk driver runs into it? (Our range was at the end of a dead-end road.)

That's not the half of it. I was fronted transportation, ammo, and registration for instructor school three times in the 1980s. In the 1990s, I sometimes got company time off and bore the expense myself. I took one wide-ranging class of six days in length that cost $1,000 just in registration. I got the time off for that one. I left for it only a few days after burying the rangemaster for whom I had worked for 15 years.

If I dollar'ed out every bit of training with all the travel, meals, ammo, and other expenses, I could actually afford to pay my health insurance premiums now. And I'm a comparative piker. I know several trainers of the Topeka Police Department whose combined training costs could have purchased that agency another helicopter!

It's not a job for lightweights. If you've had all your training paid for by the outfit, more power to you. I'm glad. I think it's the way it should be. For many of us, it's not that way. If you want in the life, suck it up. It's one of the costs.

Politics

I was surprised to see a sergeant give orders to captains and lieutenants on the range. The chief deputy at the time put complete operational control of the range on his firearms instructors. They didn't abuse that privilege and used their power to ensure everyone's safety.

I also witnessed a change in administrations and saw old grudges settled. It seemed that we'd have a few years of good, hard training, there would be a change of power, and then there would be no training. "But we qualify four times a year!" Qualification isn't training. A boss found a source that said differently, but you could call a limousine a little yellow school bus—that doesn't make it so.

I've seen people whose only desire was to make training the best it could be but who were vilified in staff meetings, treated to stony memos alleging laziness, and about whom it was said that a large amount of training was just being recommended so the instructor could be away from the brass—another yellow school bus, also perpetrated by desires for revenge.

Suck it up if you want to be in the life. It's not always good—but when it's good, it's great.

Success

Dealing with success is hard. That's because real, demonstrable success is so rare and we get little practice. I was nearly completely unaware of it for years. I'm not referring to someone saying, "That was a good class," "I learned a lot," and so on. That's nice, but it isn't on the level of real success.

I recall we did a considerable amount of training on contact weapon assaults one year. Deputies were generally stunned with what they found out but things quickly reverted to the "It can't happen to me" disease. One morning, I'd come in for a patrol day shift and a night-shift officer wanted to see me in the back room. He quickly ran the situation down: he'd pulled over to check a pedestrian on a highway, the guy was unresponsive to most verbal commands and kept his hands hidden. The officer was surprised to see this guy approach his car after being told to stop and stay. The officer gave repeated commands to stop and the guy continued his approach.

"I remembered the knife stuff we did and there was no way I was letting him get close to me," he said. Having been unable to broadcast his situation and location due to other radio traffic, he dropped into the car, put it in reverse, and backed down the highway. The subject watched this, then continued his approach. After backing several times and finally getting in on the radio, he stopped the car and got behind it.

I think the command he gave the subject was along the lines that "If you take another step, you're dead" or something like that. The subject stopped. The repeated command "Let me see your hands" yielded first one empty hand, having it return behind his back and the other hand, now empty, appearing. This silliness went on for a bit when the subject threw something into the weeds in the ditch.

Other officers soon arrived and the subject was put in custody. The officer went out in the weeds and collected a very large knife (which he showed me) partly in a sheath.

"I thought it was a gun assault," he said. "I didn't think 'knife,' but there it was."

What do you think our midnight stroller was going to do with that knife, hiding it from the officer as he walked purposefully toward him? What would have happened had this clown tried it with an officer who hadn't yet made it to in-service?

I was with that kid for nearly four hours into my shift as he erupted into full-blown logorrhea, the seemingly unending and rapid talking of someone who has just faced what he or she believed to be a near-death experience. And it was a near-death experience for him. We see it all the time with crime victims, accident victims, and in post-shooting trauma.

He kept thanking me. I had no idea how to respond. It was a situation I had never prepared for. All I could think to say was, "Are you sure you're all right? I'm glad you made it. Good job." In retrospect, I think that was the only relevant response. Ensure your officer is okay, tell him you're glad he's okay, and tell him he did fine.

Investigations

We haven't room for a complete rundown on managing officer-involved shooting investigations. If you want a class in that, contact Lethal Force Institute (http://www.ayoob.com) and see when they can get Mas Ayoob to come in to do his one-day class on that topic. It's a good one.

Having written the force policy for my agency a few times, I was called in on a couple of shootings before I was in detectives. You may be called on to do the same. A few things are noteworthy.

One is to understand that an officer can't just calmly sit and write a report in the immediate aftermath of a lethal confrontation. The information you get that way will be pretty useless. Even if the officer is outwardly calm, that isn't how things are inside. I recommend 12-24-48-hour plans. We do things on 12- and 24-hour increments. One is to allow the officer a minimum of 12 hours, more like 24 hours, before pen goes to paper. We do need some information in the extreme short term: Are you sure that you're all right? How many offenders were there? Was anyone else around? Show me about where you were and show me about where you think the offender was—things of that order. This bit of information we need to have at the scene unless the officer is incapacitated and can't talk.

We also need to get pictures of the officer as he or she is as soon as we reach the station, taking particular note of physical injuries and damaged gear and clothing. We get pictures of physical injuries again at 12 hours, 24 hours, and 48 hours. Injuries that look extremely minor often gain color over a period of hours. The officer isn't injured? Take a photo anyway, proving that the officer was in uniform—if he or she was—at the time of the shooting.

Understand that, unless your state or your agency has modified the federal standard, the officer had to use objectively reasonable force; it doesn't have to be the best choice, nor is he expected to be shot at before he can return fire.

Also, keep the officer away from the media but let him call home. The people at home should notify his lawyer. Someone in the grip of post-shooting trauma doesn't need to be left to answer media questions.

If you have an interest in this area, I'll again refer you to www.ayoob.com for more information. Mas Ayoob has informational videos there and he still offers his six-day Deadly Force Instructor school. As a graduate, I can recommend the class without reservation.

Loss

While it doesn't happen to all of us, we do have to face the possibility of losing a student. We're sending them out there with guns; we should expect it can go badly. We can experience some rough times. It's possible you may have to deal with feelings of personal failure, to be working with agency members who feel uncertainty and grief, to be held responsible by family members and the agency head.

If you feel like you failed, like the officer's loss is your responsibility, it's time to step back and look at the whole picture. It's natural to feel bad, but grief isn't solely about guilt. There are a lot of reasons this tragedy happened. Some might have to do with a lack of training, but you can't force the agency to train adequately. Even if you had the power to force a chief or sheriff to train these troops all the time, some of our students would rather take a beating than a shooting or defensive tactics class. It's not your decision who they hire or how much training they get. It's also not your decision who dies and when. That decision is made above your pay grade, so you better get used to it. For those who've worked the beat in Iraq, Afghanistan, and other garden spots, you have the advantage in this situation. You, probably better than anyone, know the pain and sorrow of loss.

Life is dealing with loss. So deal with it. You can't hide from it. Talk to other instructors, military vets who've been there. Use your array of firearms instructor contacts. Who's dealt with this already and how did he or she make it through?

Sometimes you just have to talk it all out with someone. When I lost my range boss, friend, and training partner, I descended into depression. Before that, my assessment of depression was, "Oh, feel depressed? Cheer up!" It doesn't work that way.

I didn't try everything, but it seemed to me like I had. Finally, I got to spend some time with Vince O'Neill, a world-class firearms and defensive tactics trainer. He's faced his own tribulations and he counseled me for some time. With his help, the depression passed. We can help each other out. We have to want help and have to go the extra step to get it. Don't fail this test.

Dealing with agency grief amounts to the same problem multiplied by the number of officers and the feelings of "that could have been me" that everyone feels and no one expresses. This requires grief counseling on a level that fire and EMS departments have used for years. Want more information on their methods of dealing with the grisly tragedies they routinely face? Ask them. They're more than happy to help out. They are truly brothers and sisters of the shield.

Mas Ayoob tells the story of an FBI firearms instructor, a superb trainer and, at the time, the dean of the FBI's gun school. He was on the road and was near a city where a murdered FBI agent was being laid to rest. He found out that the agent being celebrated and his partner had gone to interview a bank robbery suspect. They knocked at the door, their jackets buttoned over their sidearms. The door flew open and they were both shot to death before they could get to their guns.

The instructor elected to go to the funeral. When he arrived at the church, hushed whispers identified him. "That's 'the Gun,'" they were saying. He was at the casket, looking down at a young man too soon gone when he felt small hands tearing at him. He turned to see a woman wracked with grief.

"You're the gun teacher?" she asked, sobbing. He could only nod when she slapped him. "Son of a bitch!" she cried. "Why didn't you save him?"

He didn't tell her that he'd never met the deceased—at that time, the FBI consisted of several thousand agents—and that, if he had, he would never have taught him to call on bank robbery suspects with his jacket buttoned over his gun. None of that would matter to her. It didn't matter to him. What mattered was the loss of a young agent.

That's exactly what you can face. It's not pleasant but it is what it is.

The only thing that counts is getting back on track. Get your people ramped up to face their battles. Make sure they are equipped and trained the best you can. It's an uphill battle. It's always an uphill battle. You are fighting the administration, the governing body (budget), the local citizens (noise complaints at the range), and even fighting the officers themselves. When the worker comp claims come in from people shot with Sims rounds during simulations training, you begin to wonder if it's all worth it.

Then someone comes in and tells you that something he learned saved his life.

Network

You'll be cursed at home for thinking only "guns and law enforcement." It's the life we chose. There will be little time at work to reach out to other trainers—which leaves off-duty time to catch up. Don't just teach "what we teach here" because "that's the way we always taught it." Incestuous training is usually crap.

When I first experienced the Internet back in the early 1990s, I used it to correspond with other firearms instructors. One of the first things I got was the Clarkstown (NY) Dim-light Qualification Course. We couldn't shoot it the way they did—they have an indoor range and can adjust the light. Our range with its outdoor lighting worked okay at night. I used that course of fire up until the time I retired—just because I liked it. Besides, it met my training needs. It was one of the courses that people expressed a liking for—not a common thing where I'm located.

That was my first experience with networking over the Internet. Kansas firearms instructors now have a group on Yahoo. Greg Block of California has the LEGUN Instructors list, not always lively but always interesting when there is traffic. IALEFI has a members-only message board on their website and there are often requests for assistance and information as well as personal opinion and controversy.

The Massachusetts Association of Law Enforcement Firearms Instructors and Armorers (http://www.mlefiaa.org/) has a good website and has a Firearms Instructors' Course Manual for sale to members and nonmembers on CD. It is only available for sale to law enforcement officers. Aside from courses of fire from lots of different agencies, training courses (such as night fire) and electronic forms are part of this manual.

While outreaching through IALEFI, your state's firearms instructor group, and the Internet, you may want to check to see what the next-door neighbor is doing. I got so many good ideas from trainers at the Topeka Police Department while I was next door at the sheriff's department that it wasn't funny. We worked together closely, though our bosses often didn't, and we were working toward the same objectives. I bet your neighbor agencies have some of the same issues you do in your agency. Pick their brains.

Seminar Format

This book wasn't written to change any minds, though it was written to stake out some positions. If the material has engaged, enraged, or forced you to think about something uncomfortable to think about, good show! If not, if you've agreed with everything I've written here—then you are me. I've never met a firearms instructor who agreed with me 100%.

Use this book as a springboard to write lesson plans to refute, support, or simply to try what was represented here. Write that article you've been meaning to write. We need to hear what you have to say—that's how I got started in this crazy business. You have something to offer, so let's hear it. Let's attend your class at the IALEFI Annual Training Conference. Perhaps you are a member of ILEETA, the Chicago-area-based International Law Enforcement Educators and Trainers Association? Present there or at least write an article for their periodical.

This is a "seminar in a book," not a textbook. Use it in that way and help to find the "right" answers for all of us.

Index

A

B

C

D

E

F

I

J

L

M

N

R

S

U

V

W